MAKE LEARNING INEVITABLE

MAKE LEARNING INEVITABLE

Unveiling a Novel and Counterintuitive
Learning Paradigm for Students in the 21st Century

Rishabh Kasarla

Birmingham
Rhazes, LLC.
2024

Copyright © Rishabh Kasarla 2024

All rights reserved. No part of this publication may be reproduced, distributed, or transmitted in any form or by any means, including photocopying, recording, or other electronic or mechanical methods, without the prior written permission of the author, except in the case of brief quotations embodied in critical reviews and certain other noncommercial uses permitted by copyright law.

Published by
Rhazes, LLC.
Birmingham, AL 35209
USA

ISBN 978-0-9967761-8-9
Printed in the United States of America

Thank You:

To my mentees for joining me on this journey and giving me your trust - Akhila Nalluri, Isabella Garcia, Ishan Patel, Khushi Mehta, Youssef Ibrahim.

To Dr. Mohammadali Shoja for providing me with so many opportunities.

To Dr. Stephen Ely for inspiring me to publish this book.

To my Dad for teaching me how to think and dream big.

To my Mom for always believing in me.

I DEDICATE THIS BOOK TO THE PEOPLE WHO ALWAYS STRIVE TO BECOME BETTER.

Table of Contents:

0. Introduction 13
    0.1 My Learning Journey 13
    0.2 Audience Orientation: Is This Book Right for You? 18
    0.3 Maximizing Your Experience: How to Use This Book? 23

1. Traditional vs New Learning Paradigm 27
    1.1 Understanding Traditional Learning: Limitations and Challenges 27
    1.2 New Learning Paradigm: The Conceptual Framework 34
    1.3 Comparing Learning Paradigms: Traditional vs The New Approach 44

2. Innovation in Learning: Application Before Comprehension 57
    2.1 The First Step: Deeply Understand the Problem/Challenge 59
    2.2 Emphasizing Action: The Importance of Immediate Application 79
    2.3 Practical Techniques for Applying New Information 80
    2.4 The Power of Context and Purpose in Accelerated Learning 82

3. Confusion, Questions, and Hypotheses: The Trio of Constructive Learning 87
    3.1 Unearthing Foundations: Identifying First Principles 88
    3.2 Embracing Confusion: The Value of Discomfort in Learning 98

3.3 Navigating Uncertainty: Harnessing the Power
of Confusion and Questioning 100

3.4 The Cycle of Hypothesis Creation and Refinement:
A Catalyst for Learning 106

4. Primed for Knowledge: Preparing the Brain's 'Shelf' for Learning 113

4.1 Creating a Cognitive Appetite:
The Need for Knowledge 114

4.2 Setting the Stage for Assimilation:
Establishing Context and Purpose 116

4.3 Embracing Errors: The Role of Mistakes in Learning 118

5. The Learning Journey: Making Knowledge Acquisition Inevitable 121

5.1 Specific Goal-Oriented Challenges:
Catalysts for Active Learning 122

5.2 Designing Effective Challenges - Practical Examples 124

5.3 Learning as a Natural By-Product of
Completing the Challenge 128

6. Harnessing the Power of AI in Modern Education ... 131

6.1 General advantages of using AI in Education 132

6.2 How to use ChatGPT in the New Learning Paradigm 133

6.3 Preparing for the AI-Driven Educational Future 138

7. Transforming Yourself 143

This page is intentionally left blank

Introduction

My Learning Journey

My journey to become the best learner I could be began about ten years ago when I entered high school. As a high school student, I often struggled academically. I found myself caught in a repeating cycle: I would fall behind, push myself to catch up, only to burn out and fall behind once more. This left me incredibly frustrated, especially when facing the challenge of simple high school tests. I was particularly daunted by subjects like history, which I found dense and difficult. When I would receive my grades, I felt compelled to hide them from my peers, many of whom were exceptionally bright. I distinctly remember scoring a 40% on my first test - I felt defeated. Despite this setback, I resolved to improve and dedicated a week to intense study. However, this approach proved unsustainable, and I soon found myself struggling once again.

Around the same time, while watching television with my family, I encountered a program called "Superhumans" on Fox. The show featured individuals claiming to possess extraordinary abilities, showcasing their talents before an audience. One episode featured John Graham, the reigning memory champion of the USA, who demonstrated a remarkable feat. He accurately

INTRODUCTION

memorized detailed information from tags worn by twenty sprinters as they raced past him. Each tag contained a five-digit number, a color, and the name of the runner. Graham's ability to recall every detail, including the ability to list the numbers both forwards and backwards and answer specific questions about the runners with perfect accuracy, struck me as beyond human capability.

What truly caught my attention was Graham's assertion that memory skills like his could be learned and developed by anyone. As a student who struggled with memorization, this revelation was eye-opening. Inspired by Graham's incredible skill and his belief in the potential for anyone to enhance their memory, I resolved to embark on a journey to improve my own memory skills.

After I dedicated two years to rigorous training, I managed to achieve the same memory feat that John Graham displayed on TV. I advanced to a level where I could memorize a deck of cards in under a minute, 150 random words within 15 minutes, 100 names with faces in 15 minutes, and 600 digits in a span of 30 minutes. My efforts led me to compete in the USA Memory Championship, where I not only reached the finals, but also secured a place among the top 10.

An intriguing aspect of my journey unfolded during the final round of the championship. With only ten finalists left, the organizers asked us to share our unique paths to the competition. Given that the USA Memory Championship remains relatively unknown and tightly knit community, they were curious about how we had discovered it. When it was my turn, I recounted how John Graham's appearance on television had sparked my interest and determination to reach this level of competition. Remarkably, the very individual who had inspired my journey was one of my competitors. Competing alongside Graham was a surreal experience. Through this event, I not only achieved a

INTRODUCTION

personal milestone but also formed a friendship with him, further enriching my memorable adventure in the world of competitive memory.

This story might seem uplifting, but it serves to highlight a significant challenge. My commitment to enhancing my memory was driven by a lifelong ambition to pursue a career in medicine. Understanding the immense volume of information required in medical school and recognizing the critical importance of this knowledge for patient safety, I viewed memory improvement as a crucial skill. However, my first exam in medical school did not go as planned, despite my thorough preparation and seemingly comprehensive knowledge.

This experience led me to a crucial realization, which is the focus of this book: the mastery of memory alone is not the key to success in medical school, or in any field. The traditional belief that we must be vessels of information, capable of recalling facts and figures on demand, is a misconception. There is a more effective approach to learning and applying knowledge, one that transcends mere memorization. In this book, I aim to explore and discuss this alternative method, challenging the conventional wisdom and sharing insights into a more profound and efficient way of learning.

This discussion is not about conventional study methods or techniques. I won't be advising on the use of the Pomodoro technique, the Feynman method, or suggesting study intervals with short breaks. Nor will this conversation revolve around focus strategies or innovative note-taking methods like mind mapping. Instead, the essence of this book lies in the exploration of mindset and strategic approaches towards knowledge and information processing.

The primary objective is to delve into the ways we perceive and engage with knowledge, aiming to shift our conventional thinking patterns. By redefining our understanding of the role and nature of knowledge, we can significantly transform our learning process. This book seeks to address and transform our learning methodologies to suit the modern educational landscape, acknowledging that traditional learning methods may not fully equip us for today's challenges.

In the past, the rarity of information bestowed value upon knowledge retention, making information hoarding a valuable skill. However, in an age where a smartphone can access a vast array of information instantly, the mere possession of knowledge no longer equates to a lot of value. The real merit lies in critical thinking and the ability to apply knowledge thoughtfully. This book aims to guide the reader towards a more effective and critical approach to learning, fitting for the modern era where information is abundant and the ability to use it is invaluable.

This book focuses on educational strategy, specifically on effective ways to interact with information. The method I'll discuss aims to effortlessly boost your information retention. More crucially, it's designed to develop your abilities into those of a critical and efficient thinker, transforming the way you process and utilize information.

Rethinking Learning

During my final year of college, I faced a puzzling situation that many students might find relatable. Despite hours spent diligently reading, the knowledge seemed to evaporate once the book was closed, leaving me unable to articulate the key points I had supposedly learned. This disconnect between reading and understanding was both surprising and frustrating, highlighting a gap in my learning process.

Contrastingly, my experiences outside the academic world told a different story. Whether organizing fundraisers, practicing guitar, delivering presentations, performing magic, or playing chess, the knowledge and skills I acquired seemed to embed

INTRODUCTION

themselves naturally through the act of doing. These activities underscored a critical insight: real learning often occurs as a side effect of engaging deeply with an activity that utilizes the knowledge in a meaningful way.

This insight became even more pronounced during my early years in medical school, a domain where theoretical knowledge directly impacts human lives. The transition from absorbing information to applying it in practical, life-critical situations revealed the limitations of rote memorization. It became clear that the essence of education is not merely to amass knowledge but to develop the ability to think critically and apply that knowledge effectively.

This realization led to a profound shift in my approach to learning. I began to see each academic subject, not as an end, but as a way to develop versatile problem-solving skills. From learning organic chemistry to rare medical conditions, the content was less about the specifics and more about honing the ability to think and reason in diverse scenarios.

Embracing this new perspective, I experimented with various techniques to refine my approach. This journey revolutionized my approach to learning, transitioning from a passive intake of information to a dynamic process where learning unfolds almost serendipitously.

This book is the culmination of that journey, offering insights and strategies for a more effective and meaningful learning experience. It will present a novel learning paradigm that challenges conventional approaches.

I believe this approach to learning can revolutionize the educational landscape of the 21st century, empower learners to take control of their education, and foster a lifelong love for learning. As we embark on this revolutionized learning journey, let us remember, as James Clear, the author of "Atomic Habits" said, "You do not rise to the level of your goals. You fall to the level of your systems."

To embrace this wisdom, we must craft our educational strategy and systems with intention and precision, ensuring they are robust enough to elevate our learning experiences. It's through these meticulously designed systems, tailored to harness the potential of each learner, that true transformation occurs. As we refine our systems and methodologies, we not only enhance our ability to learn but also shape a future where education is a dynamic, interactive, and deeply engaging journey for all. Let's embark on this path not just with high aspirations but with the solid foundations of well-thought-out systems that will carry us towards our highest goals.

Audience Orientation: Is This Book Right for You?

For the Life-long Learners

Life-long learners are individuals who have an insatiable curiosity and an unending desire to learn. They are the ones who yearn to explore the vast expanse of knowledge not for professional or academic requirements but simply the sheer pleasure of understanding the world around them. If this description resonates with you, this book will provide you with a fresh and innovative approach to quench your intellectual curiosity and fuel your ongoing pursuit of knowledge.

The core idea presented in this book - treating knowledge as a tool to overcome challenges rather than an end to a means - is especially suited to your learning style. This paradigm encourages you to embark on quests, to uncover layers of understanding, and to engage with real-world problems that pique your interest. Instead of amassing knowledge by yourself, you'll learn to seek out challenges, where the journey to overcome these challenges forms the basis of an integrated learning process.

INTRODUCTION

This process empowers you to contextualize the knowledge you acquire, creating a strong connection between the abstract realm of ideas and their tangible implications. By marrying your natural curiosity with the practical application of knowledge, you elevate your learning experience. Learning becomes not just about knowing, but about creating, solving, applying, and deeply understanding.

This new paradigm makes your learning journey more enjoyable, engaging, and rewarding. It ensures that the knowledge you acquire doesn't just reside in the realm of the abstract, but lives and breathes in your interactions with the world. This vibrant, action-oriented approach not only satisfies your intellectual curiosity but also enriches your life, adding depth and nuance to the way you perceive the world.

For the Students

If you're a student, no matter at what stage, high school, college, or beyond, this book has the potential to profoundly transform your perspective and approach towards learning. This new learning paradigm invites you to escape from the traditional memorization trap and engage with your education in a dynamic, meaningful, and enjoyable manner.

The challenge-based learning framework proposed in this book treats knowledge as a tool to overcome real-world problems and challenges, rather than a means to an end. This approach instills a sense of practicality in your learning process, moving it away from abstract, detached concepts and aligning it with tangible, applicable scenarios. This could be the crucial difference between viewing your education as a tedious obligation and, instead, recognizing it as an exciting journey of discovery, exploration, and practical application.

Moreover, remember that as a student, your objective extends beyond merely accumulating data, facts, and figures. It's about understanding the world around you, questioning established ideas, exploring new ones, innovating, creating, and solving complex problems. This book helps you transition your academic journey from passively accumulating knowledge to an active, engaging exploration that connects the knowledge to its practical application.

By reframing your education as an endeavor to overcome challenges and by treating knowledge as a means to an end, you transform your learning journey. You not only learn the knowledge, but you understand its purpose and its real-world implications. This approach brings your education to life, fueling your passion for learning and preparing you to solve the real-world problems that lie ahead. This book aims to catalyze this transformation, enriching your academic experience, and your future professional journey.

For the Educators

For educators, the traditional approach of dispensing knowledge in a classroom might seem efficient, but it doesn't necessarily inspire deep learning, creativity, or application. In contrast, the new learning paradigm invites your students to see learning as an active, engaging process - one where students play a leading role in their own education.

The principle of using knowledge as a tool to overcome challenges instead of it being an end goal transforms education from a monotonous exercise of rote learning to an exhilarating journey of exploration. This is inherently more exciting and engaging for students. As an educator, facilitating this shift could lead to a notable enhancement in students' motivation, engagement, and ultimately, their understanding of the subject matter.

Furthermore, this new learning paradigm provides an opportunity for educators to redefine their roles. Instead of simply transmitting knowledge, you become a facilitator, guiding students through challenges, stimulating their curiosity, and assisting them in applying their knowledge. You don't just teach them what to learn; you teach them how to learn.

Moreover, this new approach to learning is not confined to traditional educational institutions. It can also be applied in vocational training, professional development, and other forms of education. It's a dynamic and flexible learning model that can be adapted to a wide range of contexts and learners.

Ultimately, this book provides insights into how you can transform your teaching methods to create a more engaging and effective learning environment. By doing so, you're not only enriching your students' educational journey, but also setting them up for a lifetime of independent, self-directed learning.

For the Employers and Organizations

As an employer, manager, or leader in an organization, you might often encounter the challenge of keeping your workforce abreast with rapidly changing technologies, business models, and market dynamics. Continuous learning and adaptability have become the cornerstones of thriving in this dynamic environment. This is where the principles outlined in this book can be incredibly valuable.

The idea of viewing knowledge as a tool to overcome challenges aligns seamlessly with the demands of the modern workplace. Employees who adopt this learning paradigm don't just acquire knowledge for the sake of it; they acquire knowledge to solve problems and address challenges in their work. This mindset shift on the role of knowledge leads to learning that is more targeted, practical, and applicable, enhancing their effectiveness and productivity.

Moreover, this paradigm nurtures a growth mindset, fostering a culture of exploration, curiosity, and resilience. It equips employees with the ability to self-direct their learning journey, identifying their gaps and seeking out knowledge as needed. This capacity to self-regulate and adapt is crucial in a world where the nature of work and the required skills continue to evolve, which can also help to foster more innovative and adaptive teams. By fostering this learning environment, you can enhance the creativity, adaptability, and problem-solving capabilities within your workforce, ultimately strengthening your organization's competitive edge.

Whether you are responsible for employee training and development, managing a team, or leading an organization, this book equips you with the knowledge to leverage the power of the new learning paradigm to create a thriving, resilient, and future-ready workforce.

Conclusion

In conclusion, the essence of this book rests in its core message: the shift from a traditional, knowledge-centered approach to a challenge-based, application-first learning paradigm. This new paradigm places the emphasis on using knowledge as a tool to overcome challenges, rather than viewing knowledge as the end goal. In essence, it's a paradigm that positions learning as the inevitable by-product of our objective of overcoming challenges.

Whether you are a student striving to make your academic journey more engaging and meaningful, an educator looking to revolutionize your teaching methods, a lifelong learner, or an employer aiming to foster a culture of continuous learning, this book has something for you. This is not just about a new way to learn; it's about a new way to live, to grow, and to make progress in whatever field or role you find yourself in.

We invite you to delve further in this book, where we detail how you can leverage this paradigm for more efficient, curiosity-driven, and enjoyable learning. The following chapters will delve deeper into the intricacies of the new learning paradigm, offering practical strategies and insights that can be customized to your specific context and learning goals. Remember, the path to learning is not about reaching a destination, but about enjoying the journey and growing through the challenges encountered along the way.

By embracing this paradigm, we can make learning a lifelong adventure filled with curiosity, exploration, and discovery. And so, let us dive into the next section.

Maximizing Your Experience: How to Use This Book?

First, Engage with the Book's Content Actively

The most effective way to maximize your experience is to actively engage with its content. This requires immediate application and exploration. One of the core tenets of the new learning paradigm advocated in this book is that knowledge is learned best when used as a tool to overcome challenges, not as an abstract concept to be memorized, understood, and regurgitated. This suggests a practical, hands-on approach to learning that prioritizes action before theoretical understanding.

The most effective way to learn, as championed in this book, is to successfully overcome a challenge before acquiring the knowledge required for that task. This principle is not confined to a single discipline or subject area but applies across the spectrum of learning endeavors. As you read this book, take a proactive stance to apply its insights directly to your learning journey, regardless of your field.

If you're a medical student, consider solving clinical cases before you study the disease pathology in detail. For computer science students, try to create an application before delving into the intricate details of coding functions. If you're learning a new

INTRODUCTION

language, engage in conversations with a native speaker before focusing on grammar rules. Leaders, try organizing successful fundraising events before exploring leadership principles. Architecture students can experiment with building prototypes before immersing themselves in architectural principles. If you're a salesperson, why not try selling something before consulting the experts or reading sales guides? Magicians can learn and present entire magic routines before dissecting individual techniques. Even if you're learning how to swim, swim a few laps before perfecting your strokes.

Moreover, this book advocates teaching others as an effective learning strategy. When you teach someone else, you are compelled to reach a high level of understanding, identifying gaps in your knowledge. These gaps, or points of confusion, are your steppingstones towards clarity. By acknowledging your confusion, you can formulate precise questions, the answers to which will find a permanent place in your mind.

Remember that these gaps in knowledge are not setbacks, but rather triggers that push your mind to absorb information and seek solutions like a sponge. When this newfound knowledge is acquired in the context of a challenge, there's a pre-established purpose and context for the information, making it even more memorable.

Practical application should precede in-depth learning. By acting immediately upon the insights from this book, you'll cultivate a deeper understanding and retention of knowledge, transforming not just how you learn, but how you think as well. The power of this new learning paradigm lies in its application. Embrace the challenge, engage actively, and let the transformation begin. If you have read up to this point, put the book away and try to apply what you have learned so far. Don't wait for further validation of these ideas, just try them out and witness the results for yourself.

INTRODUCTION

Using the Book as an Action Guide

This book is designed to be more than just a compendium of information—it's an action guide to reimagining and reshaping your approach to learning. Keep in mind the principles and methodologies contained herein are not strict rules but flexible guidelines. They serve as a starting point, providing you with the tools to create a personalized and adaptive learning strategy based on your individual needs, context, and interests.

The true strength of this new learning paradigm focuses on overcoming challenges before in-depth learning. Challenges, by their nature, demand action and engagement. They stir curiosity and incite problem-solving, setting the stage for deep, active learning. This book is an invitation to lean into those challenges, using them as compass points to direct your learning journey. Remember, it's in the doing that the true magic of learning happens—it's where understanding deepens, connections form, and knowledge becomes part of you.

Therefore, don't just aim for intellectual comprehension; instead, seek to translate your understanding into action. Apply the principles as you read them, experiment with the methodologies in real-world contexts, and use the lessons as a springboard. Embrace confusion, ask questions, and create hypotheses. Let these actions direct your learning process and guide you towards the answers you seek.

Be proactive, adapting and personalizing the strategies to suit your unique learning journey. Remember, this book is not about prescribing a one-size-fits-all approach—it's about inspiring you to redefine your learning process, using challenge-oriented, application-first principles as a guiding philosophy. It's about turning the traditional learning model on its head, shifting the focus from passive information absorption to active problem-solving. It's about kindling your curiosity, fostering your creativity, and ultimately, unlocking your full learning potential.

INTRODUCTION

As you delve into the book, let the spirit of exploration, discovery, and challenge drive you. Turn each page with the intention of not just understanding the content but of implementing it. The aim is to catalyze action and encourage active learning. So, don't just read—act, explore, challenge, apply. The ultimate goal is not merely to change how you think about learning, but to actually transform how you learn. Your progress is measured not by the pages you turn, but by the challenges you embrace, the understanding you attain, and the transformations in your learning journey. This is the power of this new learning paradigm, and this book is your action guide to harnessing that power.

Conclusion

As you embark on this journey through the pages, it's crucial to approach it with an open and curious mind. There will be ideas that challenge traditional perspectives and norms; embrace them. Allow yourself to question, to explore, to experiment. This isn't just about absorbing new information; it's about engaging with a new paradigm of learning, experiencing its potential, and leveraging its power for transformative growth.

In the next section we will delve into a critical comparison, contrasting the longstanding conventional learning framework with the emergent, dynamic paradigm of modern learning, setting the stage for a comprehensive understanding of the shift that's reshaping education.

Chapter 1

Traditional vs New Learning Paradigm

"The essence of the powerful mind lies not in what it thinks, but in how it thinks."

- Christopher Hitchens

Understanding Traditional Learning: Limitations and Challenges

Traditional learning. We've all experienced it, haven't we? The sight of a classroom, rows of desks facing the board, students scribbling notes from the teacher's lecture, followed by long hours of studying textbooks at home, only to regurgitate the absorbed information during exams. This is the conventional, widely accepted method of learning that most of us have been a part of.

At the heart of traditional learning lies a model of cognitive development that has been a cornerstone of educational psychology for more than half a century. This model, known as Bloom's Taxonomy, was developed by a group of psychologists led by Benjamin Bloom in the 1950s. It delineates six levels of cognitive processes, each one building on the one below it in a hierarchical fashion, much like a pyramid. The pyramid begins with the fundamental and seemingly simplest cognitive process, 'Remembering', at its base.

'Remembering' refers to the first step in the learning journey where students memorize facts, basic concepts, and answers. For example, a student may memorize the multiplication tables or spelling during this stage. This is the most common form of cognitive activity in traditional classrooms and is often what is tested in many standard examinations.

From there, the taxonomy ascends to 'Understanding'. This is where learners can explain ideas, interpret, summarize, paraphrase, or classify information. They can explain in their own words what they have learned or read. In traditional classrooms, this may manifest as students being able to explain a scientific concept or a literary theme based on what they have read and remembered.

The subsequent levels of 'Applying', 'Analyzing', 'Evaluating', and 'Creating', however, represent higher-order cognitive processes. 'Applying' involves using information in new situations, such as solving problems or executing procedures. 'Analyzing' takes it a step further, breaking information into parts to explore understandings and relationships. 'Evaluating' is about making judgments based on criteria and standards through checking and critiquing. Finally, 'Creating' involves generating new ideas, products, or ways of viewing things.

While this progression from 'Remembering' to 'Creating' seems logical, a challenge arises when traditional learning structures lean heavily towards the base of the pyramid, placing an overemphasis on remembering and understanding. Consequently, students spend more time memorizing facts and less time applying the knowledge they have learned in new contexts, analyzing information, evaluating ideas, or creating their own concepts. The higher-order cognitive processes, which are essential for critical thinking and creative problem solving, often get postponed to later stages in education or are neglected entirely. This can have serious implications for the development of skills necessary for success in the 21st-century. This skewed focus on the lower end of the cognitive spectrum forms a major part of the traditional learning approach and is one aspect that needs critical examination.

The inception of the traditional model of education can be traced back to the Industrial Revolution, a period that brought sweeping changes not just in manufacturing and technology, but also in the way societies approached education. During this era, rapid industrial growth and urbanization led to a surging demand for a standardized education system that could produce an educated workforce equipped with the necessary basic skills and knowledge.

This was a time when the world saw the rise of factories, manufacturing units, and assembly lines. The structure of the workforce was shifting dramatically, necessitating an educational model that matched its needs. Thus, the traditional learning approach was birthed, a model designed to mirror the efficiency, uniformity, and predictability of the industrial age. It allowed for the organized, systematic imparting of information that was reliable, repeatable, and most importantly, scalable. The lecture format, where a teacher would transmit information and students were expected to absorb and regurgitate, became the hallmark of this approach.

At its core, traditional education centered on enabling students to acquire foundational knowledge. It championed memorization and recall of facts, creating an educational atmosphere where the amount of information one could retain was synonymous with their intelligence. During this period, the ability to remember and reproduce vast quantities of information was not only prized but was a practical necessity. Unlike the present day, where a wealth of information is readily available at our fingertips, the pre-digital era was one of information scarcity. Books and learning resources were not as accessible, and thus, storing knowledge in one's memory served an essential function.

In many ways, the traditional learning approach was highly effective for its time. It created a structured learning environment, brought consistency to the teaching process, and helped create a literate, knowledgeable society. Its effectiveness was further validated by the societal conditions where rote learning and the recall of vast amounts of information were valuable skills. Hence, the lecture format, which was the most efficient method of delivering this scarce information, became the standard method of instruction.

However, as society evolved, so did its educational needs. The very elements that made traditional education successful in the past became its limitations in a rapidly changing world. As we moved from the Industrial Age to the Information Age, the skills needed for success underwent a massive shift. This shift necessitated a critical re-examination of our historical model of education and its place in the current educational landscape.

The benefits of traditional learning are multifaceted and contribute to a well-rounded educational experience. One of the primary advantages lies in its provision of a clear structure and a defined pathway. Each step, whether it be attending classes, completing assignments, or taking examinations, acts as a significant milestone on the learning journey. This structure provides students with a sense of achievement and purpose, as they can tangibly measure their progress and witness their growth over time. By breaking down the educational process into manageable stages, traditional learning encourages students to set goals, work towards them, and celebrate their accomplishments, fostering motivation and a sense of fulfillment.

Moreover, traditional learning offers stability in the realm of education. It establishes a universal standard of educational progress that extends beyond geographical boundaries. This standardization ensures that students across different regions and institutions are exposed to a similar curriculum and set of learning objectives. As a result, educational experiences become more comparable, allowing educators, institutions, and students to gauge progress, identify strengths and weaknesses, and make informed decisions regarding further education or careers. This comparability acts as a valuable tool for evaluating academic achievement, providing a common ground for discussion, assessment, and recognition of skills and knowledge acquired through traditional learning.

In addition, traditional learning fosters a sense of continuity and familiarity for both students and educators. It builds upon established pedagogical methods and practices that have been refined over time. This familiarity can create a supportive environment for learning, where students can rely on proven educational approaches and techniques. Furthermore, it facilitates the transfer of knowledge and expertise from experienced educators to students, ensuring the preservation of valuable insights and effective teaching strategies.

While traditional learning has undeniably played a significant role in our educational evolution, the benefits come with their share of limitations. A major drawback lies in its inherent focus on lower-order cognitive processes, such as remembering and understanding, often at the expense of higher-order thinking skills. This characteristic trait of traditional education can inadvertently create a learning environment that suppresses creativity and independent thinking.

In a traditional classroom setting, students are encouraged, either explicitly or implicitly, to memorize facts and regurgitate them during exams. The pressure to score well often results in cramming sessions where voluminous amounts of information are ingested with the primary objective of reproducing them verbatim on the test. This approach, unfortunately, leaves little to no room for critical understanding, let alone application of the learned knowledge. While it may lead to temporary academic successes in terms of grades, it fails to nurture a deep, long-lasting understanding of the subject matter. Moreover, it eclipses the innate curiosity and the inherent joy of learning.

Another significant drawback of the traditional learning model is its passive nature. A typical classroom scenario under this model sees the teacher assuming the role of a broadcaster of information while the students adopt a largely receptive role. Lessons are delivered in a one-way flow, with the teacher dispensing knowledge and the students absorbing it. While this style of teaching can be effective in transmitting a vast amount of information or foundational concepts, it does not actively engage students in the learning process.

The absence of active engagement in learning can lead to a host of issues. For one, it can create a disconnect between the students and the subject matter. When students are mere recipients of information rather than active participants in the learning journey, the learning process can feel abstract and disjointed. This sense of detachment can make it difficult for students to relate the lessons to real-life situations, further reducing their ability to apply the learned knowledge.

A passive learning environment, such as the one fostered by traditional education, is less equipped to cultivate key skills that are invaluable in our modern, rapidly evolving world. Skills like problem-solving, critical thinking, creativity, and innovation are not luxuries but necessities in today's increasingly complex and interconnected society. These skills are demanded in various fields and industries and are often the difference between merely surviving and thriving in the professional fields.

However, traditional learning methodologies, in their static and one-directional nature, seldom provide ample opportunities to develop these skills. With the primary focus on rote memorization and regurgitation, the cultivation of these critical abilities takes a backseat. In such an environment, students are seldom given the chance to grapple with complex problems, dissect and analyze multifaceted scenarios, or stretch their creative thinking abilities. The absence of these experiential components of learning can result in students being ill-equipped to face the challenges and the opportunities of the modern era.

Experiential learning, which refers to the process of learning through experience and more specifically learning through reflection, also finds little room in a traditional learning environment.

This form of learning has been hailed as an incredibly effective method to ensure a deeper understanding of the subject matter and the acquisition of practical skills. Yet, the 'sit-and-get' model of traditional learning, with its emphasis on lecture and note-taking, fails to provide students with the chance to learn by doing and subsequently reflecting on their actions.

Learning must have an overarching goal that extends beyond the mere acquisition of knowledge. Of course, acquiring knowledge is a vital component of learning, but it must be complemented with the ability to effectively utilize this knowledge in practical, real-world scenarios. This dual objective is what ensures that learning is meaningful, purposeful, and ultimately, successful.

Current traditional education excels at the task of information delivery but falls short when it comes to fostering the practical application. This glaring shortcoming calls for a necessary reevaluation of our prevalent learning methodologies. We need to encourage an evolution in our approach to education, one that ensures a balance between knowledge acquisition and skill development, and that prepares learners not just to know, but to do, and to adapt in an ever-changing world.

In conclusion, traditional learning, with its structured format and universal acceptance, certainly has its merits. It has served as the foundation of our educational system for centuries, offering a streamlined pathway to the acquisition of knowledge. However, it is not without significant limitations.

One of the major challenges of traditional learning is its often-excessive emphasis on rote memorization. In this model, the process of learning is frequently reduced to memorizing facts and figures for regurgitation during exams, with little to no emphasis on understanding or applying this knowledge in practical scenarios. This approach tends to overlook the development of higher-order cognitive skills such as critical thinking, problem-solving, creativity, and independent thinking.

Moreover, traditional learning is predominantly a passive process. It often operates on a 'broadcast' model where information is transmitted from teacher to student, with limited active participation from the latter. This passive nature can lead to a disconnect between the learner and the learning material, making the process seem abstract, irrelevant, and devoid of real-life context. Such an approach can deter learners from developing a genuine interest in the subject matter, hindering their motivation and engagement levels.

As we move further into the 21st century, with its rapid technological advancements and an ever-changing socio-economic landscape, there is a pressing need for a learning paradigm that can address these limitations. We need an approach to education that brings the learner into the center of the learning process, making it an active, engaging, and applicable process.

It is with this pressing need in mind that we will explore a new and transformative learning paradigm in the forthcoming chapters. A paradigm that revolutionizes how we perceive and approach learning, making it more than just an academic obligation, but an enjoyable, fulfilling, and life-long journey.

New Learning Paradigm: The Conceptual Framework

Introduction

The previous section dissected the traditional learning system, exposing its strengths but also laying bare its limitations. We found that our age-old approach, while effective in some respects, falls short in cultivating higher order cognitive processes. These processes, namely analyzing, evaluating, and creating, are critical for individuals navigating the complexities of the 21st century. Furthermore, we noted that our education often leans towards passivity, promoting a one-way transfer of knowledge that overlooks the vitality of engagement, creativity, and independent thinking.

It is clear that a transformative approach to learning is not just desirable, but necessary. We need a paradigm shift, a fresh take on learning that propels us from passive recipients to active seekers of knowledge and values the cultivation of higher cognitive skills just as much, if not more, than the acquisition of basic knowledge.

In this section, we will delve into the conceptual framework of a new learning paradigm designed to address these gaps. A paradigm that seeks to flip the order of Bloom's Taxonomy, amplifying the importance of higher order cognitive skills. A paradigm that urges learners to start even when they're not ready, to throw themselves into challenges that demand the very knowledge they seek.

Get ready to explore a bold and transformative approach to learning, designed to empower you with not just knowledge, but also the skills and mindset to apply this knowledge.

Radical Reordering: Flipping Bloom's Taxonomy

As we delve deeper into the prospect of a new learning paradigm, it's crucial that we revisit a familiar framework: Bloom's Taxonomy. This pyramid, ingrained in the collective psyche of educators and learners, outlines a spectrum of cognitive processes. It starts at the base with 'Remembering', then ascends through 'Understanding', 'Applying', 'Analyzing', and 'Evaluating', culminating in 'Creating' at the top. Traditionally, this structure has been interpreted as a linear hierarchy, prescribing an ascending order of cognitive engagement. Education systems worldwide have largely adopted this sequence, dedicating early education to the lower order cognitive processes ('Remembering', 'Understanding') before gradually introducing the higher ones ('Applying', 'Analyzing', 'Evaluating', 'Creating').

However, a lingering question prompts us to challenge this status quo: what if we flipped this paradigm on its head?

The proposition might seem counterintuitive, even radical. But for a moment, consider the potential advantages of turning the pyramid upside down. Instead of launching the learning journey with the assimilation of basic facts and progressing slowly, (hopefully towards creative application), what if we initiated the process at the summit? What if we ignited the learning process with the challenge of creation and allowed the understanding and remembering of necessary knowledge to follow naturally and organically? This radical reordering is the cornerstone of our new learning paradigm — a paradigm that upends traditional cognitive progression.

This reordered learning paradigm espouses a "trickle-down effect." When we place the emphasis on the higher order tasks, the lower functions naturally follow suit. Consider a learner tackling the task of creating something. The very act of creation demands understanding: the learner must comprehend the principles at play, the systems in action, the mechanics that underlie the task. And to understand, the learner must remember — the fundamental facts, the foundational knowledge. Each step of creation implicitly involves the lower-order cognitive processes. The journey to completion of the task necessitates a comprehensive engagement with all levels of cognition, rendering the learning experience richer and more holistic.

At the heart of this revolutionary approach lies an unconventional concept: "starting when you are not ready." The idea might initially seem daunting or risky. However, its potential as a learning catalyst is immense. Picture a learner, standing on the precipice of a daunting challenge. This task demands knowledge and skills that they have yet to acquire. This sets the stage for a dramatic transformation. The learner's reality starts to change. Driven by the urgency of the challenge and their inherent motivation to succeed, they are propelled into a self-guided quest for knowledge.

This radical reordering aims to ignite curiosity, cultivate resilience, and foster independent thinking, equipping learners to navigate the complexity of the contemporary world. In the following section, we will delve deeper into how we can practically implement this bold approach in our pursuit of knowledge. We will explore how, by embracing challenge-oriented learning, we can revolutionize our learning journeys.

Practical Implementation: The Path of Action

After conceptualizing the radical idea of flipping Bloom's Taxonomy, the next step is to delve into the practical aspects of this shift. How do we transform this bold concept into a functional, transformative learning experience?

The answer lies in a unique approach: embarking on a path of action. In the realm of this new learning paradigm, we do not passively absorb knowledge in anticipation of future application. **Instead, we actively seek out a challenge that compels us to attain the necessary knowledge to overcome it.** In other words, we thrust ourselves into action before acquiring the understanding deemed a traditional prerequisite for it.

The idea of seeking out a challenge before being 'ready' with the required knowledge may seem radical. It presents a substantial departure from the traditional order of education. However, it provides an effective solution to the limitations of traditional learning. In this approach, the learner identifies a task or project that necessitates the knowledge they desire to acquire. The challenge is designed in such a way that the path to its successful completion requires the learner to acquire and apply the knowledge they initially set out to learn.

The most effective way to learn is by successfully overcoming a challenge before traditionally acquiring all the knowledge required for that task. This approach applies across various fields of study and disciplines. Whether you are a medical student, an engineering student, a language learner, someone interested in leadership, an architecture student, a salesperson, a magician, or even someone learning to swim, the pattern remains the same.

Engage in practical applications before diving into the specifics and details of the subject matter: Solve clinical cases before learning the disease; create apps before diving into the intricacies of coding; conversate with a native speaker before focusing on grammar rules; organize successful fundraising events before delving into leadership principles; build prototypes before studying architectural principles; sell something before consulting experts or reading sales guides; learn and perform entire magic routines before dissecting individual techniques, and swim a few laps before perfecting swim strokes. Teaching others is also a powerful approach as it necessitates a high level of knowledge, inevitably leading to identifying the gaps in one's understanding. The act of confronting gaps in your own knowledge through the challenge triggers the mind to absorb information like a sponge and to seek out solutions. The premise is that practical application should precede in-depth learning. This results in a deeper understanding and retention of knowledge.

This process redefines the very nature of learning. The knowledge you acquire is not an abstract concept stored away for a future application. Instead, it is directly tied to the immediate goal of overcoming the challenge at hand. It provides context and practical application for the knowledge, enhancing the relevance and thereby, the retention. This direct link to a purposeful context makes the knowledge more tangible, relatable, and ultimately, meaningful.

In the new learning paradigm, knowledge is no longer the end goal. Instead, it is repositioned as a tool. This pivotal shift in perspective is at the heart of the new approach. The central aim is to overcome a self-defined challenge that requires the desired knowledge for its successful completion. The pursuit of this objective then drives the learning process, with knowledge being acquired as and when it's needed. The key is that knowledge becomes a tool, not the end goal. The end goal is becoming a critical, effective, and capable thinker.

Consider an architecture student - She doesn't learn about construction materials, load-bearing calculations, and building regulations for their own sake, or to pass a theoretical exam. Instead, these pieces of knowledge become valuable tools that she needs to successfully design and construct her building. The knowledge is acquired, understood, and applied in the context of her project, making it relevant and meaningful. This purpose-driven acquisition of knowledge enhances her engagement, improves retention, and deepens her understanding. By focusing on the goal of overcoming her challenge, the knowledge naturally falls into place, seamlessly integrated into her pursuit of success.

Moreover, the path of action inadvertently catalyzes the process of learning. As the learner navigates through the challenge, grappling with obstacles, knowledge gaps, and exploring potential solutions, they encounter various learning moments. These moments are not pre-planned or structured, but rather, arise naturally out of the process of problem-solving. This spontaneous, organic learning makes the acquisition of knowledge seem almost accidental, like an unexpected, yet pleasant, by-product of the journey towards resolving the challenge.

Embracing the path of action positions learners as active explorers, not just passive recipients of knowledge. They become investigators, intimately engaging with the material, analyzing, and applying it in meaningful ways. This approach transcends using just cognitive processes; it's a holistic journey engaging both the mind and emotions.

Challenges naturally push learners beyond comfort zones, igniting curiosity, fueling excitement, inducing occasional frustration, and ultimately yielding satisfaction upon completion. These emotional experiences drive learning, enhance retention, and build resilience, grit, and a growth mindset — critical traits for lifelong learning and success in the 21st-century world.

Therefore, this immersive approach elevates learning beyond an intellectual exercise to a transformative experience. Learners are not merely acquiring knowledge; they are also developing essential cognitive, emotional, and possibly even interpersonal skills. This enriching, holistic method embodies the full potential of what learning can be in the new paradigm.

By focusing on the challenge, we instill purpose and context into the learning process. We shift from rote memorization to meaningful comprehension, and from passive reception to active exploration. This transformation of the learning journey brings us one step closer to realizing the potential of the new learning paradigm.

Choosing the Challenge

Choosing the right challenge is paramount. The challenge serves as the vehicle through which learning takes place, thus it must be tailored to your learning objectives while taking into account your current skill level, interests, and the resources available to you.

The first and perhaps most critical criterion for selecting a challenge is its alignment with the end-goal of the desired knowledge. The challenge must simulate real-world applications of the knowledge or skill you intend to acquire. For example, if your aim is to learn architectural design, your challenge could be to create a model of a sustainable building, incorporating the latest green technologies. If you venture into medicine, you might volunteer at a local clinic or immerse yourself in solving medical cases/problems. An aspiring engineer might embark on building a robot or designing a software solution. By simulating the end-goal of your learning, the challenge enhances the relevance and applicability of the knowledge acquired, providing a clear context for how it might be used in the real world.

The second criterion is specificity. A well-crafted challenge must be concrete, with a clearly defined goal and a definitive endpoint. This offers a tangible target for the learner, providing both motivation and direction for the learning journey. A vague or nebulous challenge can leave the learner floundering, unsure of what is required or how to achieve success. A clearly defined challenge, on the other hand, provides a roadmap, guiding the learner's actions and decisions throughout their journey.

Thirdly, the chosen challenge should be designed in a way that allows for feedback. Feedback, in this context, pertains to a system or mechanism that provides information about the learner's performance relative to their goals. This could be in the form of test scores, self-evaluation, peer review, or guidance from a mentor or expert in the field. Feedback is integral to the learning process because it allows the learner to gauge their progress, understand their strengths and shortcomings, and adjust their approach accordingly. A challenge that lacks a feedback mechanism leaves the learner in the dark about their performance, impeding learning, and growth. Moreover, feedback, whether it's self-generated or from an external source, is vital in aligning one's learning strategy and ensuring that the knowledge acquisition is on track. Self-feedback is a reflective process, enabling learners to evaluate their performance against the standards and outcomes they set for themselves at the outset of the challenge. External feedback, on the other hand, offers a different perspective, providing valuable insights that the learner might have overlooked.

In essence, the right challenge is one that closely simulates the desired end-goal, is specific, suitably complex, and provides a system for feedback. By fulfilling these criteria, the challenge becomes a powerful tool that not only facilitates the acquisition of new knowledge but also contributes to the development of a myriad of other essential skills such as problem-solving, critical thinking, and self-regulation.

The Practical Implications of the New Learning Paradigm

The transition to this new learning paradigm incites a transformation in the educational journey, with significant practical implications that resonate across disciplines. To illustrate this, let's follow the journey of an architecture student.

The Learner's Role and Learning Process: In this new paradigm, the architecture student evolves from merely memorizing textbook material to actively applying their knowledge. For instance, the student might learn about architectural styles by designing a virtual tour through significant architectural periods. This immersive task requires the student to acquire knowledge about various styles, their distinctive elements, and historical context. This way, they actively participate in their education, turning learning into a deeply engaging and purposeful experience.

Learning Activities and Assessment: Instead of traditional lectures and exams, the paradigm promotes experiential learning activities. The architecture student could be tasked with designing a small-scale model of a sustainable building. This task necessitates learning about materials, structural integrity, and environmental impact in a real-world context. Simultaneously, assessment becomes an integral part of the learning process. The student receives continuous feedback on their model design, providing them with ongoing insights and allowing them to fine-tune their knowledge and skills.

Learning Environment: Under this new paradigm, the learning environment extends beyond the walls of the classroom. The architecture student might get involved in a local community project, such as helping design a park pavilion. Through this real-world task, the student learns about local regulations, community engagement, and practical project management, enriching their understanding and application of architectural principles.

In essence, this new learning paradigm reimagines education. By turning learning into an active, contextual, and reflective process, it empowers learners like our architecture student to take control of their education, nurturing a lifelong love for learning and preparing them to effectively navigate their professional paths.

Conclusion

In conclusion, it is evident that this new learning paradigm represents a transformative shift in our approach to education. By flipping the traditional structure of Bloom's Taxonomy and focusing first on higher-order cognitive skills, we have established a radical, yet pragmatic, strategy for learning. This new approach, underscored by taking on challenges, allows for learning to occur almost accidentally, embedded within the journey towards achieving a larger objective.

In an innovative twist on traditional learning models, we embrace a methodology where challenges dictate the learning trajectory, propelling us towards the acquisition of requisite knowledge. This dynamic approach involves selecting a task or project so intrinsically linked to the desired knowledge that the journey to its completion guarantees learning. Here, practical application takes precedence, flipping the conventional sequence of learning on its head and positing that the most profound understanding stems from action before we are ready.

Knowledge, in this context, transforms from a mere objective into a vital tool to solve problems and overcome challenges. As learners immerse themselves in this process, every hurdle and gap in understanding becomes an opportunity for growth, ensuring that learning moments are not just encountered but actively sought and embraced in the quest for solutions.

Throughout this section, we have underscored the practicality of this new paradigm, as illustrated by our example of an architecture student. This active, context-oriented approach to learning nurtures a robust connection between knowledge and its application, engendering a deep, immersive, and meaningful learning experience. Moreover, the emphasis on feedback enables a continuous, dynamic process of improvement, ensuring that learning remains aligned with the learner's goals.

It's important to underscore a fundamental paradigm shift that this book promotes: Knowledge, contrary to the common saying, is not power in of itself. It is potential power. The true power resides in the application of that knowledge - to create, solve, and apply to real-world scenarios. Knowledge hoarded and unutilized remains dormant, it's like a seed that hasn't been planted. The seed has potential, but without being planted and nurtured, it fails to grow and produce. Similarly, knowledge must be used, tested, and applied to unleash its full potential. That's when it transforms from being a mere potential power to an active one, driving innovation, solving complex problems, and propelling you towards personal and professional growth.

As we move forward, we will delve deeper into the mechanics of this new paradigm. We will also investigate the ways this approach can be leveraged to maximize learning efficiency, sparking curiosity, enhancing enjoyment, and most importantly, cultivating lifelong learners.

In the next section, we will contrast this new paradigm with traditional educational models, shining a light on its advantages while addressing potential challenges.

Comparing Learning Paradigms: Traditional vs The New Approach

Introduction

As we have delved into the transformative new learning paradigm in the previous sections, it's now essential to provide a comparative lens to help understand its profound implications. In this section, we aim to juxtapose this new approach against the traditional learning paradigm, dissecting and analyzing both to unearth their core differences.

The purpose of this comparison is not to undermine the significance of the conventional methods, which have undoubtedly served us for decades. Instead, our intention is to illuminate the strengths and opportunities inherent in this new paradigm, while acknowledging the challenges that this radical shift may present.

In the spirit of continuity and to facilitate a more nuanced understanding, we will continue to draw parallels and delineate contrasts through various examples. Through this comparative exploration, we hope to provide a comprehensive understanding of the transformative power of our proposed paradigm, positioning it as not just an alternative, but a compelling advancement in the realm of learning.

Key Differences: Traditional vs. New Paradigm

As we delve into this comparison, it is crucial to understand that the traditional and the new paradigm represent different approaches to learning.

Role of the Learner:

In the traditional paradigm, the learner often assumes a passive role, absorbing information transmitted by the teacher. This model views learners as empty vessels to be filled with knowledge. In contrast, the new paradigm positions learners as active constructors of knowledge. They're not simply passive recipients of information, but they actively engage with it in a meaningful way. For instance, our aspiring architect doesn't begin by simply memorizing building principles; instead, she is thrust into a real-world project where she applies these principles before formally learning them. She forms her own hypotheses, tests them, and gains feedback, thereby actively constructing her understanding of the architectural field. In this way, the learner in the new paradigm learns the principles as she thinks for herself, interacting with the knowledge and making it her own.

Learning Sequence:

In traditional education, learning follows a linear, bottom-up sequence. It starts with the foundational knowledge, the building blocks, before gradually moving towards more complex applications. For instance, a computer science student in the traditional paradigm would first learn programming languages, algorithms, and data structures before venturing into the development of a software application.

In contrast, the new paradigm places the application or the challenge at the center of the learning process. A learner might start with the objective of developing a specific software application, and this challenge, drives the acquisition of foundational knowledge and skills. Instead of laying a foundation of knowledge before attempting to apply it, the learner plunges directly into a challenge that necessitates the understanding and application of this knowledge.

In the process, the learner uncovers the need for specific knowledge and skills and acquires them as part of the journey towards overcoming the challenge. It's like reverse engineering the learning process. The problem-solving, the decision-making, the innovating required to meet the challenge - all these involve active exploration, reflection, and application, leading to a deeper, more personal understanding.

This challenge-driven learning sequence enhances the practicality and relevance of knowledge as it ties it directly to real-world application. It makes learning an exciting journey of discovery and problem-solving, increasing engagement, and often accelerating the acquisition of knowledge and skills.

Context of Learning:

Traditional education often imparts knowledge in isolation. Take for example, a medical student in the traditional paradigm. They may spend hours memorizing anatomical facts in isolation, without understanding how these facts apply to medical diagnosis or treatment. This isolated approach can lead to knowledge that is fragmented and lacks relevance or applicability.

The new learning paradigm shifts this by embedding knowledge within its practical context right from the start. Imagine the same medical student. Instead of beginning with isolated anatomy facts, they might start with a case study - a patient presenting with a certain set of symptoms. The challenge then becomes to diagnose and propose a treatment for this patient.

As the student navigates through this case, they would naturally encounter the need to understand certain aspects of anatomy - perhaps the functioning of the heart to interpret the patient's symptoms, or the musculoskeletal system to comprehend the implications of a particular symptom or the impact of a certain treatment. The pursuit of a solution to a real-world problem like this inherently establishes a meaningful context for the anatomical facts that need to be learned.

This realistic context not only gives relevance to anatomy facts but also offers a practical application of how they come into play in actual medical scenarios. It makes the learning journey engaging and much closer to the real-world tasks a doctor undertakes. This enhances both the understanding and retention of knowledge, as well as the readiness to apply it in actual medical practice.

Feedback Mechanisms:

Traditional educational systems often emphasize grades and standardized tests as the primary means of feedback. This focus encourages rote memorization and cramming to achieve short-term performance, often at the cost of deep understanding and long-term retention. The score on a test becomes the goal, rather than a real understanding of the knowledge and its application.

Consider the example of a budding salesperson enrolled in a traditional sales training program. In such a program, feedback may come in the form of an end-of-course examination, evaluating the trainee's knowledge on sales techniques and theories. The trainee might cram the night before, managing to recall the material sufficiently to pass the test, but without developing a deep understanding or the ability to apply these techniques in a real situation. Moreover, once the test is passed, the information is often quickly forgotten because it was never fully understood or integrated.

In contrast, the new paradigm promotes feedback that is immediate, ongoing, and directly tied to the application of knowledge. In this paradigm, our salesperson might begin their learning journey by taking on the challenge of selling a product or service. Feedback would come in the form of customer responses, sales numbers, and insights from experienced mentors. Every customer interaction would provide an opportunity to apply, test, and refine their sales techniques.

The nature of this feedback allows the salesperson to gauge their progress in real time and adjust their approach. They would learn sales techniques as tools to achieve their goal, making them meaningful and applicable. This approach provides a deep understanding of the sales process, equipping them with the practical skills needed to succeed in the real world of sales.

In the new learning paradigm, feedback is not a judgement but a tool for growth and improvement. It guides the learner's journey, helping them to adjust their course as they go, and ensuring that the learning remains directly tied to the application of knowledge.

Motivation for Learning:

In the traditional paradigm, knowledge acquisition often becomes the primary focus. Learning is seen as an end in itself, with the material to be mastered for its own sake or for potential future use. This perspective can sometimes lead to learning that feels abstract and disconnected, as its relevance or application may not always be immediately apparent. This paradigm can also lead to motivation that is largely extrinsic - driven by factors such as grades, approval, or avoidance of failure.

An example of this is a traditional math class, where a student might learn formulas and principles primarily because they will be on a test, with little consideration of their real-world relevance. This can result in learning that feels detached and inapplicable, contributing to a lower level of engagement and retention.

However, in the new paradigm, the motivation for learning shifts fundamentally. It reframes learning from being an end in itself, to being a powerful means to an end. The aim is not merely to learn for the sake of learning, but to learn to overcome a self-selected challenge, to solve a real problem, or to achieve a specific goal.

Picture an aspiring engineer who decides to build a working prototype. The motivation here is not just to acquire knowledge on circuit design, materials science, or software programming. Instead, the motivation is to build a functional prototype, and the required knowledge becomes the means to that end. The engineer learns the knowledge not because they need to pass a test or get a grade, but because they need the knowledge to build their device. This way, learning becomes meaningful, relevant, and highly motivating.

The motivation, in the new paradigm, stems from the aim of overcoming a specific challenge. It's no longer about acquiring knowledge for the sake of knowledge or for some future application. Instead, it's about utilizing knowledge as a tool to directly achieve a tangible outcome, making learning an engaging, meaningful, and purpose-driven process. Almost as a by-product, the learner becomes deeply connected with the knowledge, leading to higher retention and an enriched understanding.

These key differences provide a starting point. By focusing on real-world examples and how these two paradigms operate in various scenarios, we will further appreciate the implications of these differences.

Addressing Potential Concerns with the New Paradigm

The new learning paradigm, while promising, may raise several concerns. Some might question the feasibility of implementing this approach in traditional educational settings or worry about the learners' ability to choose and navigate challenges. Others might worry about ensuring comprehensive knowledge coverage. In this section, we will address these concerns and offer potential solutions and mitigations.

Feasibility of Implementation:

Implementing the new paradigm on a large scale presents significant challenges, especially when compared to the more linear, structured approach of the traditional paradigm. The new learning approach is, in many ways, a radical departure from standard educational practices, and to implement it requires a fundamental shift in pedagogical strategies and institutional structures.

The new learning paradigm resembles more of an independent learning process, wherein the learner takes the reins of their educational journey. Such learner autonomy can seem daunting to systematize on a larger scale due to the diverse array of challenges for each learner. Institutions would need to accommodate a multitude of learning paths, each differing based on the unique challenge selected by the learner.

Moreover, the existing structures of traditional education - discrete subject-based curriculum, standardized assessments, fixed schedules - are largely incompatible with the dynamic, integrated, and personalized nature of the new paradigm. These systemic barriers make the large-scale implementation of the new paradigm challenging.

However, these challenges are not insurmountable. Several schools and universities around the world are already making strides towards implementing aspects of this new paradigm. They are introducing flexible curricula that allow learners to define their learning objectives and pursue challenges that interest them. They are also adopting mentorship-based models, wherein educators serve more as guides or coaches rather than purveyors of knowledge, facilitating learners in their self-directed journey.

Problem-based learning (PBL) is a prime example of this shift. PBL is an instructional method used in many disciplines, although it is most prominently utilized in medical education. It presents students with complex, real-world problems, often in small groups. The essence of PBL is that the learning process is driven by the problem itself – it is the starting point of the learning journey.

In PBL, students engage in self-directed learning, guided by the problem at hand. The problem serves as a trigger to stimulate learning and to drive the acquisition of knowledge. For example, a medical student presented with a complex patient case might have to learn about relevant aspects of human anatomy, physiology, and pathology to understand and manage the case effectively. The motivation for learning in PBL comes from the need to understand the situation, making it engaging.

PBL, while innovative in its approach, stops short of fully embracing the principles of this new learning paradigm. In PBL, the problems are designed to guide students toward learning specific content areas and to trigger critical thinking and provoke questions. However, the engagement often ends there. The goal is to explore these problems and extract learning points, but the emphasis remains on the knowledge itself, rather than on specific applications.

In contrast, the new learning paradigm goes beyond posing questions and problems. It involves overcoming specific challenges where the knowledge the learner wants to gain becomes a necessary tool for overcoming these challenges. The challenge is specific to the knowledge needed and is created for the final usage case of the knowledge. This is a subtle but profound difference. In PBL, the problem is a means to an end—the end goal being knowledge acquisition. In the new learning paradigm, the specific challenge is the objective, which is tackled first, and knowledge acquisition is the means to accomplish this objective. The end goal is to become a critical, effective, and capable thinker. This flipping reframes learning, shifting the emphasis from passive absorption of information to active application of knowledge in pursuit of a goal.

While PBL represents a significant shift toward more practical, problem-oriented learning, it does not fully embody the principles of this new learning paradigm. The journey towards transforming our learning systems is a gradual one. PBL is a step in the right direction, offering valuable insights and lessons for further evolution.

Despite these challenges, the feasibility of implementing the new learning paradigm should not be dismissed. It necessitates a shift in thinking about education and demands flexibility, innovation, and a departure from traditional norms. Yet, with the promise of fostering a more meaningful, engaging, and effective learning experience, the pursuit of such change seems not just feasible, but necessary.

Choosing and Navigating Challenges:

Choosing and navigating challenges is a critical aspect of this new learning paradigm that warrants further discussion. Unlike traditional learning models, where the path of study is predetermined and uniform for all learners, the new paradigm places a significant amount of responsibility on the learner. This is seen in their ability to identify appropriate challenges that align with their learning goals, as well as to navigate these challenges effectively to extract the requisite knowledge and skills.

The task of selecting appropriate challenges may seem daunting to learners who are accustomed to prescribed curricula. However, this skill, like any other, can be developed with time and experience. It requires learners to have a clear understanding of their learning goals, an assessment of their current knowledge and skill levels, and an appreciation for the kind of tasks that will lead to the acquisition of the desired knowledge. This involves a fair amount of introspection and self-assessment - knowing what they don't know, so to speak.

Furthermore, navigating through these challenges requires adaptability, resilience, and resourcefulness. Learners must be prepared to encounter difficulties, make mistakes, and revise their approaches considering feedback. This process of trial, error, and adjustment is an integral part of the learning journey and fosters a growth mindset - the belief that abilities can be developed through dedication and hard work.

Importantly, the process of choosing and navigating challenges also hones vital metacognitive skills. Metacognition, often referred to as "thinking about thinking," involves being aware of one's own thought processes and being able to regulate them effectively. It encompasses skills such as self-reflection, strategic planning, and self-monitoring. By selecting their challenges and devising strategies to overcome them, learners are, in effect, training these metacognitive skills, which are vital for independent learning and problem-solving. The new learning paradigm not only facilitates the acquisition of specific knowledge but also cultivates essential skills for lifelong learning.

Therefore, while choosing and navigating challenges might be a hurdle for some learners initially, it is a critical skill that gets honed as part of the learning process. This not only ensures that learners gain the knowledge they seek but also fosters their growth as autonomous, adaptable, and reflective learners, ready to navigate the complexities of the real world.

Comprehensive Knowledge Coverage:

The concern about comprehensive knowledge coverage is valid. Critics argue that by focusing on specific challenges, learners may neglect or overlook important areas of knowledge that don't immediately apply to their current task. However, in the new learning paradigm, this is addressed by the careful design and selection of challenges.

In this paradigm, challenges are not random or arbitrary. Instead, they are deliberately curated to necessitate the acquisition of the desired knowledge. Each challenge is crafted to require a specific set of skills or understanding for its successful completion. Through this process, the learner is ensured to gain the necessary knowledge in a meaningful and applicable way.

However, a single challenge may not be sufficient to cover the entirety of a complex subject. Multiple challenges can be curated to collectively necessitate the acquisition of the full range of required knowledge. The learner's journey then becomes a collection of interconnected challenges, which can become one comprehensive challenge. This approach ensures that learners are exposed to and acquire all necessary knowledge, without sacrificing the relevance and applicability that characterizes this new learning paradigm.

Moreover, the mentor or guide plays a significant role in this journey. Their role extends to more than just providing guidance; they ensure that learners are exposed to a diverse range of challenges, each requiring a different set of knowledge and skills. Self-guidance is a core part of this new paradigm, allowing learners to be the curators of their own learning journey.

An essential point is the depth and richness of understanding learners gain in this paradigm. The specific knowledge areas they do focus on are explored actively and constructively, resulting in a level of understanding that often surpasses the breadth of shallow knowledge typically acquired in traditional education.

The new paradigm, therefore, addresses the need for comprehensive coverage not by enforcing the rote memorization of a set curriculum but by presenting a challenge that demand a broad and deep understanding of the subject matter. The outcome is a learning journey that is both comprehensive and meaningful, where knowledge isn't merely collected, but understood, applied, and remembered. This approach promotes not only the acquisition of knowledge but also the development of critical skills like problem-solving, creativity, and adaptability, ultimately preparing learners for real-world challenges.

Conclusion

In conclusion, the traditional and new learning paradigms present two fundamentally distinct approaches to learning, each with its unique features and implications. The traditional paradigm views the learner as a passive recipient of information, emphasizes a linear, one-size-fits-all learning sequence, and often places knowledge in isolated contexts. Feedback in this system are generally tied to formal assessments, and the driving force for learning comes from the end goal of mastering the knowledge.

In contrast, the new learning paradigm positions the learner as an active explorer of knowledge, learning by directly engaging with challenges that require the knowledge they aim to acquire. This paradigm reverses the conventional learning sequence: the challenge drives the acquisition of foundational knowledge and skills, rather than being the culmination of the learning process. It places learning within meaningful contexts, offers ongoing and nuanced feedback, and fosters intrinsic motivation from the objective of overcoming challenges to achieve the end goal of becoming a critical, effective, and capable thinker.

This shift from traditional to new paradigm is not without its hurdles. Concerns about the feasibility of implementation on a large scale, ensuring comprehensive knowledge coverage, and learners' ability to choose and navigate challenges are valid. However, with strategic design, careful planning, and perhaps most importantly, a mindset shift, these challenges can be mitigated.

The new learning paradigm holds transformative potential. By redefining the role of the learner, the sequence of learning, the context of learning, the nature of feedback, and the motivation for learning, it promises a more dynamic, engaging, and effective learning experience. It equips learners with not just specific knowledge and skills, but also the metacognitive abilities necessary for lifelong learning and problem-solving. By leveraging this paradigm, we can make learning a truly empowering process, deeply connected with real-world challenges and personal growth.

Chapter 2

Innovation in Learning: Application Before Comprehension

*"If you wait till you are ready, it will be too late.
Learning starts with immediate action."*

This chapter introduces a radical yet effective learning method we call, "Application Before Comprehension." The term may initially seem paradoxical — how can one apply something they have not yet comprehended? Isn't comprehension the prerequisite of any kind of practical application? In conventional learning models, indeed it is. However, the approach in this book challenges that presumption, advocating a shift in the learning paradigm that has the potential to revolutionize how we learn and teach.

What is 'Application Before Comprehension'?

The concept of "Application Before Comprehension" revolves around the notion of active engagement with tasks and challenges prior to thoroughly understanding the underpinning theories. It implies that learners dive into practical problems, start working on them, and through that process, identify the knowledge they need to acquire. This approach contrasts the traditional model in which learners first consume theoretical knowledge passively and then apply it later. The knowledge can often lack a real-world context or relevance to an immediate need or purpose.

Origins and Inspirations

The "Application Before Comprehension" model is deeply rooted in educational theories like experiential learning, problem-based learning, and constructivist learning. These theories emphasize the importance of active learning and context, advocating that learners construct their own knowledge through experience and reflection. They highlight the importance of problem-solving, critical thinking, and authentic tasks, ideas that have served as a strong foundation for our new learning approach.

Indeed, the idea of "Application Before Comprehension" draws upon a concept which isn't entirely new. Over the years, educators and theorists have acknowledged and advocated the importance of higher order cognitive skills, as outlined in Bloom's Taxonomy. They have emphasized engaging with these higher levels, namely analysis, evaluation, and creation, as early as possible to deepen understanding and foster critical thinking.

A notable proponent of such an approach is Justin Sung M.D., an educator who shares his insights on his popular YouTube channel. He suggests learners to engage in higher order functions of Bloom's Taxonomy in their learning process to promote a more dynamic and active understanding of the material. In these methods, learners engage in high levels of cognition after they've acquired an adequate level of theoretical knowledge.

What sets "Application Before Comprehension" apart from standard active learning approaches is its more radical perspective. This approach goes beyond just involving higher order cognitive skills early on; it goes as far as to say these activities should be engaged in *before* acquiring theoretical knowledge about the topic. The learner begins their journey not by understanding, but by doing, tackling tasks that require high-level cognitive skills from the start. This is the innovative leap that forms the foundation of the method we'll delve into in this book.

My personal learning journey is a testament to the power of this strategy. When I began to experiment with different learning strategies, I started engaging with tasks higher up in Bloom's Taxonomy earlier and earlier in the learning process - directly applying my knowledge, analyzing problems, and evaluating solutions before I'd fully comprehended the underlying theory. Eventually, I decided to go radical: to start at the top of Bloom's pyramid, creating, synthesizing, and evaluating before even acquiring knowledge.

This was a groundbreaking experience. I found that starting higher on Bloom's Taxonomy, even before acquiring knowledge, sparked my curiosity and engagement. It directed my learning, focusing it on the most relevant and fundamental aspects of the topic. It also made learning much easier and more enjoyable, as I was not just passively consuming information, but actively applying it, seeing its relevance, and observing its impact. This profoundly changed my perspective on learning, and it formed the basis of the method discussed in the following chapters.

In the first section, we will delve into the first step of the process: deeply understanding the problem or challenge at hand. This step is crucial, as it sets the stage for the entire learning process and primes your brain for efficient and effective learning.

The First Step: Deeply Understand the Problem/Challenge

Thought Experiment

Imagine you are student who just started trade school. You want to become a builder, you just started school and you have no prior experience - you don't even know what a hammer is. Just go along with it. Imagine on the first day that you are given a block of wood and a nail, and you're given a task: to drive a nail into a piece of wood. Now consider three different learning paths that you might approach this task:

1. You're handed a comprehensive book about hammers: how to use them, how they're made, their history, and the physics behind their use. It even includes an exhaustive chapter on the variety of nails you might encounter. After reading through the book, you make sure that you understand all of the details by reading it over and quizzing yourself. Eventually, after you feel confident enough you decide to use the hammer.

2. You're simply given a hammer and the nail and told to "figure it out." You start off by observing the hammer and its properties and decide on different ways to use the hammer. You then decide on the best and most efficient way to use the hammer based on your prior experience and through testing the different methods.

3. You're shown the nail and the piece of wood but not given any tools or instructions. You're left to ponder the challenge, to question, to explore possible solutions. Eventually, you realize that the only way to drive the nail into the wood is by using *something* that can hit the nail hard enough and fast enough so that it can pierce the wood. You have an idea of what needs to be done in order to complete the task, but not sure what can fulfill this role. At this point, you might ask if there is a tool with a heavy end that you believe might be able to provide enough force and power to drive the nail into the wood.

Which of these three scenarios do you think would lead to the most effective learning experience?

The third scenario, where you're left to ponder the challenge of driving a nail into wood without tools or instructions, is likely the most effective for learning. It fosters active engagement, critical thinking, and creative problem-solving right from the start. By not providing immediate solutions, it encourages you to deeply understand the task at hand, explore various possibilities, and recognize the need for a specific tool, leading to a more profound and practical grasp of the subject.

A student in the third scenario might look something like the following:

You're standing in a room with a piece of wood and a nail. The goal has been clearly defined - drive the nail into the wood. There are no tools in sight and no one to guide you, the problem is all you have in front of you.

You begin by closely examining the problem. You hold the nail, feeling its sharp point and flat head. You tap it against the wood, observing how the wood is too hard for the nail to penetrate by hand. You think about the need for force, something that can strike the flat head of the nail hard enough to drive it into the wood.

You know that the only way to drive the nail into the wood is to apply a force high enough and quickly enough. You need something that can accomplish this basic function. Even if you never heard of a hammer before, you find yourself craving something like a hammer, not because it's part of a curriculum, but because you genuinely need it to solve your problem.

Now, imagine the moment you're finally given the hammer – analogous to getting the knowledge. It's not just a piece of information anymore; it's a solution, a means to an end. The knowledge you are given after fully understanding the problem and after understanding the purpose of knowledge is a solution that will contribute to completing a challenge.

You know exactly what the purpose of the hammer is. You grasp it with determination, intuitively finding the right way to hold it. You experiment with different swings, learning through each strike how to direct your force, how to aim, and how to protect your fingers. And this might take trial and error. You've started applying, analyzing, and even creating new techniques, all without a single lecture or reading.

You're not just learning about the hammer anymore. You're learning how to solve problems. And all this knowledge is being absorbed organically, almost accidentally, as you strive to complete your task. Your focus is not on learning for the sake of learning but on solving the problem at hand. Yet, by the end, you've not only achieved the original goal but also acquired a wealth of knowledge about hammers and their use. This is the crux of the "Application Before Comprehension" approach. By setting a challenge first, you're creating a genuine need for the information, which leads to more effective and engaging learning.

But why does this happen?

To appreciate the impact of the third scenario, we should understand the significance of Bloom's Taxonomy. This hierarchy of objectives starts with basic levels of cognitive engagement such as remembering and understanding, and gradually ascending to higher, more complex levels such as applying, analyzing, and creating. Traditional learning approaches align with this hierarchy by teaching new information in a sequence. This is displayed in the first scenario, where you begin at the base of Bloom's Taxonomy by reading about hammers and nails and gradually building your understanding, to finally applying it in practice.

The second scenario, though it may appear radically different, also mirrors a step in Bloom's Taxonomy - the application stage. You're handed the tools and instructed to figure out how to use them, mirroring an educational setting where you're given information and immediately expected to apply it. The process may differ from a formal classroom, but the principle is similar: knowledge is given first, then application is expected. However, in this case, the application comes much earlier than in a traditional setting.

The third scenario breaks the tradition. Instead of starting at the lower rungs of the taxonomy, you launch right from the top. You engage in evaluative and creative tasks, higher-order cognitive functions that involve problem-solving. Here, you're not applying knowledge after it's given to you. Instead, you're applying skills and information before you've acquired them, or to be more precise, you're acquiring them through the act of applying them. This active engagement with the problem at hand, even in the absence of prior knowledge about hammers and nails, brings forth a novel approach to learning that challenges conventional wisdom and promises to revolutionize the way we think about knowledge acquisition. Here is a more in-depth analysis of the third scenario:

1. Discovery and Inquiry: This approach encourages active engagement with the problem from the outset. Without being provided with a tool or explicit instructions, you're forced to think critically and creatively about how to achieve the goal. This process of discovery and inquiry fosters a deeper understanding of the problem and potential solutions.

2. Cognitive Engagement: The challenge of figuring out how to drive the nail into the wood without immediate resources stimulates cognitive engagement. You're not just learning about a tool and its uses; you're actively involved in understanding the very nature of the task and conceptualizing the kind of tool that would be required, which engages various cognitive processes such as problem-solving, analysis, and synthesis.

3. Contextual Learning: When you eventually discover or are introduced to the hammer as a solution to your problem, the learning is contextual. You understand the purpose and utility of the hammer in direct relation to a real. This contextual learning ensures a more profound and lasting grasp of the knowledge because it's tied to a tangible application.

4. Motivation and Satisfaction: The "eureka" moment of realizing what tool is needed and why it works effectively to solve the problem provides a sense of achievement and satisfaction. This emotional response to learning can significantly enhance motivation and the retention of knowledge.

5. Foundational and Transferable Skills: The process of identifying the problem, hypothesizing solutions, and testing those hypotheses cultivates foundational skills that are transferable to other learning contexts. It's not just about learning to use a hammer; it's about developing a methodological approach to problem-solving that can be applied broadly.

In essence, the third scenario embodies a more holistic learning experience. It's not just about the acquisition of knowledge, a tool (the hammer), but about developing a problem-solving mindset, fostering creativity, and engaging deeply with the learning material. This scenario most effectively utilizes the principles of active learning, where knowledge is constructed through experiences and interacting with the environment.

The strength of this approach is that it creates a learning pathway in which applying and acquiring the desired skills becomes the only option in overcoming a specific challenge. You're not just passively receiving information but actively using it. Knowledge is not the final destination, but rather, it is the tool we utilize in our pursuit of overcoming challenges. The completion of our objective lies in mastering the challenge itself. It is in the process of confronting and resolving the challenge that we cultivate a necessity for knowledge, even before knowing what that knowledge is. This necessity stirs a cognitive hunger for new information, facilitating its swift assimilation into our knowledge base. Furthermore, since the context established by the challenge provides a purpose for this newfound knowledge, we are primed to grasp it. In this paradigm, knowledge serves as the necessary tool that we acquire in our journey, while the destination remains the resolution of the challenge.

The acquisition of knowledge becomes inevitable because it's the only way to succeed in overcoming the challenge. Essentially, this approach turns the traditional learning model on its head: instead of starting with acquiring knowledge, you start with the problem, the challenge – and that's where we begin our journey of 'Application Before Comprehension'.

So, what does this all mean for you? This approach to learning sets the foundation for a problem-solving mindset. You're encouraged to apply information as soon as possible, even before you fully understand it, even before you have it. This active engagement can lead to deeper understanding, better retention of knowledge, and the development of practical, real-world skills.

The Importance of the Challenge

What is the role of the challenge? How does focusing on a high-level task rather than directly on the acquisition of information contribute to the learning process? This approach to learning does not stand alone; it demands a problem to resolve or an operation to execute. At the heart of this learning approach is the high-level task, a problem that needs resolution or an operation that calls for execution. This task isn't just a backdrop against which learning happens; it forms the very nucleus of the learning journey. As we grapple with the intricacies of the task, learning begins to flow naturally.

When engaged with the high-level task, we unravel a transformative process of learning. As we work towards task completion, every challenge encountered, every uncertainty faced, and every problem solved contribute towards our expanding knowledge base. The information and insights gained in this process aren't simply absorbed in isolation. They are intimately tied to the task at hand, enabling us to understand their practical relevance and application, thereby solidifying our understanding. This is not passive learning, but active knowledge, born out of necessity and honed by application. Importantly, confusion isn't just inevitable – it's essential. It acts as a catalyst, sparking an influx of queries, and thus, propelling the learning process forward.

Deeply Understanding the Challenge

Why deeply understand the challenge?

When faced with a problem, the initial impulse might be to jump into finding a solution immediately. However, the first and most critical step is to understand the problem deeply. Deep understanding allows you to grasp the intricacies of the problem, exposing the nuances and complexities. It's like turning on a flashlight in a dimly lit room; you begin to see details previously obscured. Hidden obstacles reveal themselves, and suddenly, unexpected opportunities start to emerge. This deep understanding lays the foundation for comprehensive, well-thought-out solutions, rather than rushed, superficial ones.

Nowhere is this more evident than when dealing with complex challenges, ones that involve multiple moving parts and interconnected elements. Without a deep understanding, you're akin to a puppeteer with tangled strings, unsure of which tug will lead to the desired action. Having a deep understanding helps you identify the relationships among these elements, untangling those strings, and providing a strategic guide towards effective problem-solving. Moreover, it equips you with the insight to foresee potential outcomes and implications of various solutions. This predictive capacity reduces the risk of unintended consequences, ensuring your solutions are not just effective in the short-term, but also sustainable in the long run.

Consider a doctor diagnosing and treating a disease. Truly understanding the problem is the first step in treating it. If a patient comes in presenting symptoms such as fatigue, fever, and recurring headaches, a superficial approach would be to prescribe treatments for these symptoms individually. However, by deeply understanding the challenge - truly understanding the symptoms and identifying the root cause of the symptoms and how they are related - the doctor would employ a comprehensive approach, taking a detailed medical history, ordering lab tests, and analyzing the data. This might lead to a diagnosis of a rare form of anemia, which were the initial symptoms. Truly understanding the problem is the first step in treating it.

With this in-depth understanding, the doctor can create an effective treatment plan, addressing the root cause rather than the symptoms, prescribing specific medications, dietary changes, and closely monitoring the patient's health. In this scenario, the deep understanding not only leads to a correct diagnosis but also an effective treatment plan, ultimately leading to better patient outcomes.

Approaching learning begins with a thorough understanding of the challenge at hand, akin to deciphering a complex puzzle. This understanding acts as a compass, guiding you through the maze of information, ensuring that your learning efforts are targeted and relevant. Consider a chef learning to perfect a complex dish. The chef's deep dive into each ingredient's role, cooking techniques, and the science behind flavors provides a clear roadmap. This clarity not only directs their practice and study but also sparks curiosity, leading to questions like, "Why does acidity balance richness?" or "How does slow cooking enhance depth in the dish?"

Moreover, this deep understanding anchors learning in real-world contexts. For a student building a solar-powered car, abstract principles of photovoltaics and aerodynamics become tangible and directly applicable. Concepts that once seemed distant and theoretical now have immediate practical applications, aiding retention and comprehension.

Ultimately, this approach transforms learning into an active journey. Instead of merely absorbing information, you're critically engaging with it, much like a detective piecing together clues to solve a mystery. Each piece of new knowledge is examined, questioned, and pieced together into your growing understanding of the challenge. This active engagement not only makes learning more effective but also more meaningful, as you see the direct impact of your growing knowledge on solving real-world challenges.

How to deeply understand the challenge

To "deeply understand" a challenge implies immersing oneself into the core of the problem, grappling with its intricacies, and absorbing its nuances. It is not a superficial scan of the issue but a comprehensive dive into its essence. This deep understanding unfolds in three interconnected stages - deconstructing and simplifying the problem, identifying the initial and desired states, and recognizing the transformations required to bridge the two. This process encourages questioning the unclear, envisioning the successful outcome, and strategizing the learning pathway. By committing to this deep understanding, learners not only comprehend the breadth of the challenge but also appreciate its depth, providing them with a robust foundation to explore solutions and learn effectively.

In the journey to deeply understanding a problem or challenge, learners navigate through three crucial, interconnected stages. Before delving into the intricacies of each, I will first outline a broad overview with an illustrative example. Subsequently, I will explore the significance of each stage, along with the methods and mindsets that underpin each, to ensure a thorough comprehension of this process.

Let's start with an example to delve into each stage and look at the steps.

Challenge: An architecture student is tasked with creating a bridge.

Stage 1: Understanding the Challenge

Understanding the Problem: The student begins by outlining the primary objective of building a bridge, focusing on its purpose (e.g., connecting two landmasses, facilitating traffic flow) and considering key factors like location, terrain, and environmental impact.

Deconstruction and Simplification: The bridge project is dissected into smaller, more manageable segments:

- Purpose and Functionality: Determining whether the bridge is for pedestrians, vehicles, or both.
- Geographical Considerations: Assessing the area over which the bridge will span, such as a river or valley.
- Environmental Factors: Evaluating potential environmental impacts and challenges posed by local weather patterns and water flow.

Incisive Questioning: For each segment, the student poses targeted questions to refine their understanding and identify potential hurdles, such as, "What materials are best suited to withstand local environmental conditions?" or "How will the bridge design integrate with existing transportation networks?"

Identifying Gaps in Knowledge: The student reflects on their current expertise and resources, pinpointing areas requiring further research or skill development, like advanced structural engineering principles or knowledge of sustainable building materials.

Stage 2: Identifying Current and Desired States

Current State Assessment: The student takes stock of available resources, existing knowledge, and any preliminary designs. This phase involves a realistic appraisal of the student's own capabilities and the project's detailed presentation and starting point.

Defining the Desired State: The envisioned outcome is a structurally sound, aesthetically pleasing, and functional bridge that meets all specified requirements and integrates seamlessly into the surrounding environment. Success metrics might include safety, durability, design innovation, and environmental sustainability.

Outlining the 'Problem Space': The gap between the current capabilities and resources and the envisioned bridge project is mapped out. This 'problem space' encompasses the learning and development needed to acquire new skills, knowledge, and resources essential for the project's completion.

Stage 3: Planning the Transformation

Developing Strategies: The student formulates overarching plans to guide the project to completion. Strategies may involve sequential phases of design, testing, and construction; partnerships with engineering experts; and engagement with local communities and environmental consultants.

Determining Steps: Concrete steps are laid out, such as:
- Conducting detailed site surveys and environmental impact assessments.
- Developing preliminary designs and models for testing and feedback.
- Securing necessary materials and resources, adhering to budgetary and timeline constraints.

Implementing Tactics: Specific, actionable measures are adopted in relevant contexts to advance the project. Tactics might include utilizing simulation software for design testing, organizing community feedback sessions, or initiating pilot construction phases to assess feasibility.

By methodically navigating these stages, the architecture student sets a clear path from the initial concept to the realization of the bridge project, ensuring that each step is aligned with the overarching goal of creating a functional and impactful structure.

Following this example, let's transition to dissecting the dynamics and details of each stage, and unraveling how they interplay to foster a profound comprehension of any given problem or challenge.

The **first stage** of deeply understanding a problem is all about **deconstructing and simplifying the challenge**. Consider this stage as akin to dismantling a complex machine into its basic parts, examining each piece closely, and understanding its purpose and function. Complex scenarios are broken down into their constituent parts. This is not merely a process of disassembly; it also involves recognizing the relationships. Could there be causation, correlation, or perhaps a more complex dynamic at play? This exploratory exercise helps make the seemingly insurmountable challenge more manageable and logical.

Incisive questioning is at the heart of this stage. Learners are urged to probe every aspect that is unclear, to be the detective who relentlessly pursues the truth. Like a detective gathering clues, learners scour every detail, no matter how small or seemingly insignificant, to understand the bigger picture. They engage in an incisive dialogue with the problem, posing thoughtful questions and seeking comprehensive answers. It is very important that there be a thirst for clarity and a refusal to move forward until the ambiguity is minimal. There is no room for assumption or speculation. If something doesn't make sense, if a piece of the puzzle seems out of place, questions should be raised. This is not about obtaining all the answers immediately; it's about recognizing the right questions to ask.

An essential part of deeply understanding a challenge is confronting the question: "What do I not know? This question serves as a powerful mirror, reflecting the gaps in our understanding and knowledge. It invites humility and openness, reminding us that it's not only okay to not know everything, but it's also a necessary condition for learning and growth. Tackling this question can be unsettling, but it helps in delineating the known from the unknown, thus revealing the areas that require further exploration. Additionally, it encourages curiosity and inquiry, prompting us to seek answers, explore different perspectives, and embrace the learning journey. By recognizing and articulating what we do not know, we take a significant step towards deepening our understanding of the problem at hand.

A useful barometer to measure understanding at this stage is the learner's ability to explain the problem in everyday language. If one can't explain it simply, then one doesn't understand it well enough, as Albert Einstein famously said. A complex problem explained in simple terms is a testament to deep understanding. The result is a clear, comprehensive, and nuanced picture of the challenge, which acts as a road map, guiding learners towards effective solutions. This stage equips learners with a rich understanding, illuminating the intricate facets of the problem and providing an efficient path to resolutions.

Here is an example of the first stage with a medical student faced with a patient who presents with shortness of breath, a cough, and a fever. To deeply understand the patient's condition, the student begins by deconstructing these symptoms, much like dissecting a complex mechanism into simpler components.

1. Deconstruction and Simplification: The student breaks down the complex presentation of a patient's illness into simpler, individual symptoms, such as isolating shortness of breath to lung or heart issues, identifying a cough as lung irritation, and recognizing fever as an immune response. This process makes the overall problem of diagnosing more manageable by identifying key areas - lung or heart problems, lung irritation, and activated body inflammatory response.

2. Incisive Questioning: The student delves deeper into each symptom with precise questioning, exploring the underlying mechanisms and relationships between them. They question the nature of shortness of breath, the causes and mechanics of a cough, and the physiological basis of a fever, seeking to understand how these symptoms interrelate and how they tie back to the patient's history and potential lung infections like pneumonia. This is about going deep and finding what you do not know about the information that is being presented.

3. Identifying Gaps in Knowledge: The student reflects on what information they lack with their current level of knowledge, broadening their inquiry beyond the presented symptoms to consider additional relevant factors. This introspection uncovers areas for further learning, such as the specifics of pathogens causing similar symptoms or the distinguishing features of different lung infections, highlighting the need for a more comprehensive understanding of the medical condition. This is about going wider with your inquiries and finding what you do not know about the information that is not being presented. Notice the contrast with the previous point.

4. Explaining in Simple Terms: The student's goal is to articulate the patient's condition in straightforward language. If they can explain that the patient might have pneumonia, characterized by an infection in the lungs leading to inflammation, fluid accumulation, and the observed symptoms, they demonstrate a deep understanding of the problem at hand.

In diagnosing a patient, a medical student methodically deconstructs complex symptoms into simpler components, engages in detailed questioning to understand underlying mechanisms and relationships in the presentation, and introspectively identifies their own knowledge gaps to build a comprehensive understanding of the condition. Through this process, the medical student transforms a daunting diagnostic challenge into a clear, approachable problem, setting the stage for effective treatment planning and further learning.

The **second stage** of deeply understanding a problem takes the lens of understanding and sharpens its focus on the **current and desired states of the challenge**. In every challenge, there's a point of origin and a goal; grasping both thoroughly is crucial for resolution. The essence of resolving the problem lies in transitioning from where we are to where we aim to be. This stage serves for finding and truly understanding the starting point and setting the destination.

Recognizing the current state of affairs is the starting point. Here, the learner evaluates and takes stock of what already exists. It's an exploration and understanding of the present conditions. What is the nature of the problem as it currently stands? What factors contribute to its existence? What has been done so far to tackle it, if anything? This is akin to assessing the terrain before embarking on a hike – observing the lay of the land, spotting potential hurdles, and appreciating its distinctive characteristics.

Once the current state has been comprehensively assessed and understood, the next step is articulating the desired state, painting a vivid picture of the solution. What is the outcome that we want to achieve? How do we define success in this specific context? What does the 'finished product' look like? It's about establishing a vision of the future, a projection of where we aim to be that serves as the standard against which progress will be measured.

Understanding these two states – the current and desired – is vital, as they essentially outline the 'problem space.' This is the gap between 'what is' and 'where we aim to be.' It defines the journey to be embarked upon, it is the void that learning seeks to fill. It is in traversing this space that the learner will transform the current state into the desired state, effectively bridging the gap through the acquisition of skills and knowledge or translation of knowledge into actionable steps.

In the case of our medical student analyzing a patient's condition, the second stage involves a keen focus on the patient's current health status and the ultimate goal of treatment.

Current State Assessment: The medical student thoroughly evaluates the patient's current condition. They take into account the presenting symptoms—shortness of breath, cough, and fever—and gather more data through physical examination, patient history, and possibly diagnostic tests like chest X-rays or blood work. This step is akin to mapping the terrain before a journey, understanding the patient's health landscape, including any underlying conditions, the severity of the symptoms, and how they impact the patient's daily life.

Articulating the Desired State: With a clear understanding of the patient's current condition, the medical student then envisions the desired outcome of the treatment. This could be the complete resolution of the infection, the disappearance of symptoms, and the return of the patient to their normal daily activities. The desired state is a patient who is symptom-free, with clear lungs on the X-ray and normal blood markers, indicating the body is no longer fighting an infection.

Understanding the gap between the current state (a patient suffering from symptoms indicative of pneumonia) and the desired state (a healthy, symptom-free patient) sets the stage for the medical student's learning journey. It highlights the knowledge and skills they need to acquire to effectively bridge this gap—understanding the most effective treatments for pneumonia, the typical course of the disease, and how to monitor the patient's progress towards recovery.

This stage outlines the problem the medical student needs to navigate. It defines the learning objectives: to understand the pathophysiology of pneumonia, the standard treatment protocols, and the criteria for recovery. Each step the student takes in their learning journey—from studying antibiotic regimens to learning about supportive care measures—is a step towards transforming the patient's current state into the desired state of health.

The **final stage** of deep understanding zooms in on the **necessary transformations** that must occur to transition from the initial state to the desired state. Essentially, **making a plan** to move from the current state to the desired state. This is the culmination of the previous stages, where learners are tasked with identifying what needs to change, and how it can change, to arrive at the desired outcome.

In the first part of this stage, the learner develops strategies. Strategies are overarching plans that guide us toward the desired end state by considering the overall scope of the problem, what resources we have, and any obstacles we might face. This might involve considering the order in which steps should be taken, how to manage time and resources, and even how to mitigate risks. Coherent ordering involves understanding the connected layers of overarching strategies as well as the sequence of transformations in the logical progression of steps from the current state to desired state. The formulated strategies serve as the learner's roadmap, guiding their way towards the desired state.

Next, learners grapple with the steps that must be taken. They must question what exact actions need to occur to facilitate the shift from the current to the desired state. What transformations need to take place? What new skills need to be acquired? What behaviors need to change? What knowledge needs to be gained? What processes need to be put in place? What moves need to be made? What needs to change? Each step represents a milestone on the journey towards the final goal, and understanding these steps forms the building blocks of the transformation.

Grasping the broad strategies and detailed steps paves the way for identifying targeted tactics. These tactics are deliberate, precise actions that actualize the strategies within the right contexts, catalyzing substantial progress. Executed in the appropriate environments, these tasks and activities propel the transformative process forward.

By understanding these transformations, learners can then formulate a strategic action plan, effectively mapping out their pathway from the present to the future. This action plan outlines the route to be taken to traverse the 'problem space' of the challenge. It's not about just knowing where you're going but knowing exactly how to get there.

In the context of our medical student transitioning a patient from suffering from pneumonia to being healthy again, the final stage of deep understanding involves formulating a comprehensive treatment plan.

Developing Strategies: The student begins by developing an overarching strategy for treatment. This strategy accounts for the full scope of the patient's condition, including any comorbidities, the severity of the pneumonia, the patient's medical history, and potential risks or complications. The strategy might include prioritizing immediate relief of severe symptoms, such as using oxygen therapy for shortness of breath, while also considering long-term recovery such as antibiotics to clear the infection. The student assesses the resources available, i.e., hospital facilities, medication, and the patient's support system, alongside potential obstacles like drug resistance or patient non-compliance.

Identifying Necessary Steps: With a strategy in place, the student then breaks down the necessary steps to achieve the desired state. This might involve initially stabilizing the patient, administering the first dose of antibiotics, scheduling follow-up tests to monitor progress, and planning patient education for home care post-discharge. For example, the student realizes that to reduce the patient's fever and alleviate discomfort, antipyretics like acetaminophen can be administered, and for the cough, a cough suppressant or expectorant. They understand that antibiotics are crucial for tackling the bacterial cause of pneumonia and that the choice of antibiotic might depend on whether the pneumonia is 'community-acquired' or 'hospital-acquired'.

Formulating Tactics: Finally, the student focuses on tactics— distinct, actionable measures taken in precise contexts that implement the overarching strategies, yielding significant progress. In managing pneumonia, specific tactics applied in precise settings are key. Administer antibiotics immediately upon diagnosis to start combating the infection efficiently. Monitor vital signs closely after medication to quickly identify any adverse reactions. Schedule follow-up tests like chest X-rays, post-antibiotic admin, to evaluate treatment effectiveness and adjust plans accordingly. Lastly, provide clear discharge instructions on medication adherence, symptom monitoring, and prevention strategies to empower the patient for self-care and minimize reinfection risk. Each tactic, applied in its relevant context, advances patient care significantly.

By meticulously planning the journey from the patient's current state of pneumonia to the desired state of health, the medical student uses their deep understanding of the problem to guide their actions. This plan acts as a roadmap, detailing not just the destination but also the specific routes, potential detours, and milestones along the way, ensuring a structured and informed approach to patient care.

Finally, each of these stages offers a layer of depth to understanding, collectively leading to a profound grasp of the challenge. This process of deconstruction, visualization, and transformation planning equips learners to tackle complex problems with an informed, focused approach. It fosters a deep understanding that goes beyond surface-level recognition, setting learners up for effective problem-solving and meaningful learning experiences.

By adopting this approach, we're not only acquiring knowledge but also developing essential problem-solving skills and honing our ability to apply knowledge. It lays the foundation for an active learning process where the learner takes control and navigates the journey. The destination is set, but the path to get there is filled with opportunities for exploration, experimentation, and discovery.

As we explore this innovative learning approach, it's essential to recognize that it represents more than just a rearrangement of learning steps. It signifies a fundamental transformation in our learning philosophy, redefining the purpose and function of knowledge itself. Knowledge is viewed as a tool for solving problems - it is not the ultimate objective. This paradigm encourages us to engage with challenges proactively, applying knowledge in practical contexts even before full understanding is achieved. In doing so, we not only enhance our problem-solving skills but also evolve into more critical and effective thinkers. This philosophy is encapsulated in the principle of "Application Before Comprehension."

Emphasizing Action: The Importance of Immediate Application

The initiation of the learning journey begins with understanding the challenge at hand, but the real momentum builds when the learner takes action. After truly understanding the problem, and steps are taken to overcome the challenge, then the learning process is in motion.

Immediate application is essential. When action precedes knowledge acquisition, it inevitably leads to encountering gaps - moments of realization that something is missing. Consider an instance where you need to drive a nail into wood but lack knowledge about the appropriate tool. These gaps foster a sense of confusion, provoking questions and igniting curiosity. When answers arrive, either from a source material or a teacher, they immediately fill these gaps, enabling progress towards overcoming the challenge. This process stimulates a cognitive appetite for new information, which, once satiated, promotes swift assimilation of the information into our knowledge base.

If we wait until we feel fully prepared to encounter a challenge, we miss the chance to deeply root the information we're learning. Tackling a challenge only after preparation might facilitate the use of short-term memorization, but it fails to foster the deeper, more intuitive understanding that comes from grappling with a problem firsthand.

Moreover, in high-pressure situations like a stressful exam, where memorized knowledge may temporarily elude us, we are compelled to rely on our intuition and foundational understanding. This reliance on our core comprehension, honed through firsthand engagement with challenges, becomes our lifeline, guiding us through moments when detailed facts might be momentarily inaccessible due to stress.

Engaging with challenges from the outset fosters this deeper, more resilient form of knowledge, ensuring we're equipped not just with facts, but with an intuitive grasp of the subject that can withstand the pressures of stressful situations.

In this model, the learning process is inextricably intertwined with the active search for solutions. It is through the active exploration of possible solutions, the courage to experiment, stumble, adjust, and retry, that authentic learning blossoms.

This constructive, skill-building, problem-solving endeavor engages the learner deeply in the subject matter. The dynamism of this learning method not only energizes the learner but also enhances both comprehension and retention. This heightened understanding and recall occurs because the information learned becomes directly tied to real-world, pertinent challenges.

Immediate application is pivotal in learning as it unveils knowledge gaps, fuels curiosity, ensures retention, fosters intuitive understanding, builds resilience in high-pressure situations, enhances problem-solving skills, and directly ties learning to real-world challenges, making the process dynamic and deeply engaging.

Practical Techniques for Applying New Information

Applying new information effectively can take many forms but looks the same in all fields or disciplines. Here are a few examples across various disciplines demonstrating the objective and the nature of immediate application:

Medicine: (From personal experience) Medical education frequently employs simulation-based training, allowing learners to apply new information immediately, often before achieving full comprehension. Take, for instance, medical students learning about emergency response in a critical situation, like a cardiac arrest. The students might be thrown into a high-stress simulation of a patient in cardiac arrest, where they must make split-second decisions and apply treatment protocols, even if they've just been introduced to them, or not at all. The immediate application of their rudimentary understanding creates an acute awareness of their knowledge gaps and prompts them to ask pointed, practical questions about the protocol. After the simulation, they delve deeper into the theoretical underpinnings of their actions, facilitating the swift integration of their experiential learning with the theoretical knowledge. This experience, though initially overwhelming, often leads to a profound understanding of emergency protocols and the confidence to apply them in real-world situations.

Engineering: In an engineering context, immediate application might involve constructing a prototype. For instance, a mechanical engineering student studying fluid dynamics could design and build a water pump. The process of creation allows them to organically identify knowledge gaps, seek solutions, and apply theoretical knowledge in a practical context.

Business: In business and management courses, case studies are often used to apply newly acquired knowledge. A learner studying marketing strategies might be given a real-world case of a company that needs to increase its market share. The student must analyze the case, develop a marketing plan, and present it, applying theoretical concepts to a practical situation.

Art: In fields like painting or sculpturing, the application of new techniques or methods is immediate and hands-on. An art student learning about the use of light and shadow in creating depth might be tasked with creating a still life painting that demonstrates these principles. The act of painting becomes an exploration of the newly learned concept, bridging the gap between theory and practice.

Literature: A literature student learning about narrative techniques might be assigned to write a short story employing the technique of stream of consciousness. The act of writing allows the student to apply and experiment with the technique, deepening their understanding of it in the process.

The underlying thread across all these disciplines is the bias towards immediate practical application, rather than studying the theoretical knowledge itself (ex: the published protocol of what to do during a cardiac arrest or the principles on how to create depth in an artwork using light and shadow). In each field, learners are guided to immediately use the information before they fully grasp the theory, leading to a deeper and more comprehensive understanding. This active engagement, intrinsic to immediate application, allows learners to navigate the complexities of their respective disciplines effectively and organically, enhancing both learning and performance.

The Power of Context and Purpose in Accelerated Learning

What does context and purpose mean?
What does context and purpose really do for learning?
How does context and purpose facilitate accelerated learning?

Context and purpose are fundamental building blocks in accelerated learning; they shape our understanding, fuel our motivation, and catalyze the application of new knowledge. Engaging in action prior to acquiring knowledge naturally creates gaps of understanding, Then, when filled with information from a reliable source, satiates the cognitive craving for new knowledge that was stimulated by the gap. This inevitably results in rapid incorporation into our knowledge base and equipping us with the tools to continue progressing in tackling the challenge. Cognitive craving can lead to rapid incorporation because the context that the challenge provides for this new knowledge not only gives it purpose, but also primes us for its comprehension and retention. In essence, the 'power of context' relates to the environment or circumstances surrounding the learning process, while 'purpose' refers to the clear objective or goal that the knowledge serves.

The power of context in learning cannot be underestimated. When learning is contextualized, new information is embedded within a meaningful framework that mirrors real-world situations, making it easier to understand, remember, and apply. When learners can see the relevance of what they are studying, it transforms abstract concepts into tangible ideas. A mathematical formula, for instance, becomes more than a set of symbols when you understand its application in calculating the trajectory of a satellite. Similarly, understanding a complex biochemical process becomes easier when you understand its direct relevance in a disease pathology. Contextualized learning makes abstract concepts concrete by showing where and how they can be applied, anchoring them in real-world scenarios, thus providing a clear path to future application.

Purpose, on the other hand, imbues the learning process with a clear sense of direction and intent. The pursuit of a clearly defined objective provides an anchor for the learning process, orienting all efforts towards a common goal. Purpose is the 'why' behind our actions and serves as the driving force that propels the learning journey. This approach is about methodically deciphering the relevance of knowledge to specific tasks, a process rooted in logical reasoning rather than broad, motivational usefulness. It involves a detailed analysis of why and how a concept applies, laying out a direct, understandable path to its practical application in real-world scenarios.

For example, during her rounds, a medical student tries out a diagnostic technique she's not fully mastered, driven by the need to apply it in a real-world scenario. This deliberate act of applying knowledge before full comprehension is not motivated by a vague sense of usefulness but by a logical, methodical analysis of the technique's relevance to the challenge. This experience not only cements her understanding of the technique beyond what any textbook could offer but also lays out a clear, logical path for its practical application, illustrating the direct correlation between theoretical concepts and their real-world utility.

Another example: A computer science student, while developing an app, decides it is necessary to implement a complex algorithm she only partially understood. This decision isn't spurred by a broad sense of its utility but stems from a logical, analytical understanding of how the algorithm directly applies to enhancing the app's functionality. By integrating the algorithm into her project, she not only solidifies her grasp of the concept through practical application but also clearly delineates its relevance and effectiveness in a real-world setting, embodying the principle of learning through direct, logical application.

Together, context and purpose serve as powerful tools for facilitating accelerated learning. They provide the setting and motivation for learning, making it relevant and meaningful. By anchoring new information in a specific context and towards a clear purpose, learners can quickly see the implications of their knowledge and how it can be applied in practical scenarios. This dual focus on 'where' (context) and 'why' (purpose) paves the way for immediate application and deep understanding.

Chapter 2 Summary

Overview

- Introduces a transformative learning method: engaging in practical tasks before fully grasping theoretical concepts.

Introduction to 'Application Before Comprehension'

- Presents a shift in learning: engaging with tasks before fully understanding underlying theories.

- Challenges traditional models where theoretical knowledge precedes practical application.
- Draws from higher order cognitive skills in Bloom's Taxonomy, promoting early engagement with analysis, evaluation, and creation.

Implementation

- Deep Understanding: "Application Before Comprehension" starts with deeply understanding the challenge. This involves simplification, identifying what is given and what is asked, and then outlining a plan from start to end.
- Immediate Application: Action before full knowledge reveals gaps, boosting curiosity and comprehension.
- Context and Purpose: Anchors learning in real-world relevance, accelerating understanding and application.

Conclusion

- Advocates for a learning paradigm shift towards active engagement and practical application, promising a richer, more intuitive, learning experience.

This chapter lays the groundwork for a transformative learning approach where practical application leads to deeper understanding and effective problem-solving, challenging traditional educational paradigms by prioritizing active engagement with challenges.

Chapter 3
Confusion, Questions, and Hypotheses: The Trio of Constructive Learning

"The impediment to action advances action. What stands in the way becomes the way."

- ***Marcus Aurelius***

Chapter 3 takes us on a journey through a terrain often deemed uncomfortable but surprisingly fertile for learning: confusion, questions, and hypotheses. This trio forms a potent combination, crucial for constructive learning. Often, our instinct is to avoid confusion, resist questioning, and shun hypothesizing for fear of being wrong. However, in the quest for accelerated learning, we must reconsider these natural instincts and appreciate the transformative power of these elements.

Instead of shying away from confusion, we embrace it as an integral part of the learning process. By acknowledging confusion, we tap into a state of curiosity and open-mindedness that spurs questioning and forming hypotheses. This journey is not devoid of emotional challenges, and it is equally important to understand and manage these emotional aspects to successfully navigate the learning process.

From coping with the initial discomfort of not knowing to leveraging uncertainty as a springboard for questions, this chapter guides you through these turbulent waters of confusion. Eventually, you will find yourself in the dynamic cycle of forming, testing, refining hypotheses, and forming new questions — a catalyst that propels you towards finding the most fundamental truths of the discipline you are studying. So, buckle up as we dive deep into the world of confusion, questions, and hypotheses, the trio that paves the way for accelerated, constructive learning.

Unearthing Foundations: Identifying First Principles

Introduction: Defining the Goal

As we delve into the intricate dance of confusion, questions, and hypotheses in the learning process, a pertinent question arises: What is the underlying aim of engaging in this cyclic journey? The answer lies in a profound concept known as 'first principles'. First principles are the foundational truths at the heart of any concept - the bedrock of understanding upon which all other knowledge is built.

When we encounter confusion, we attribute it to encountering a gap in knowledge, a hurdle that obstructs our path to understanding. This confusion, rather than being an endpoint, is a launching pad, prompting us to ask pertinent questions that delve deeper into the roots of our understanding. These questions propel us into thinking about the deeper, more fundamental first principles that govern the subject matter at hand.

We then formulate and apply hypotheses of these deeper principles in specific, varied, and nuanced scenarios, and add additional parameters to test if these supposed first principles hold true across the board. The dynamic nature of this process allows for constant refinement, with each round of testing shedding light on the accuracy of our hypotheses and stimulating more questions.

This process isn't linear. It is iterative, cycling continuously through stages of confusion, questioning, hypothesis generation and testing. This ongoing cycle reflects the deep, explorative journey we undertake in the pursuit of uncovering the first principles. Every round of this iterative process takes us a step closer to unearthing the foundational truths of our study and achieving our ultimate goal: mastering the subject matter by understanding its first principles.

Architecture Student Example:

> Consider the architectural design of a building. An architect is challenged to design a sustainable building that efficiently uses natural light to reduce energy consumption. The confusion arises from the complexity of factors to consider in achieving this goal, like the building's orientation, materials used, structure of the spaces, etc.
>
> From this confusion, several questions emerge: How can the building be oriented to maximize sunlight exposure? What materials will effectively trap and diffuse this light without causing overheating? How can the interior be structured to distribute natural light evenly? These questions hint at fundamental principles of architecture and sustainability - the first principles that the architect seeks to uncover.
>
> The architect then forms hypotheses: a building oriented towards the sun's path may receive the most light; using reflective and transparent materials could potentially enhance natural light indoors; creating open spaces might allow for more even light distribution. These hypotheses, based on the architect's understanding of architectural principles, need to be tested.
>
> The architect applies these hypotheses in varied scenarios - using 3D modeling software, they create virtual models of the building with different orientations, materials, and interior structures, applying additional parameters like the local climate, the time of the year, etc.
>
> With every model tested, the architect gains more insight into the validity of their hypotheses, prompting more refined questions: Does the building's orientation affect natural lighting

year-round, or is the impact seasonal? Do certain materials perform better under specific climatic conditions? How does the size and shape of open spaces affect light distribution?

Through this iterative cycle of confusion, questioning, and hypotheses testing, the architect progressively uncovers the first principles of sustainable, light-efficient building design. This process, while demanding, ultimately equips the architect with the knowledge to design buildings that harness natural light efficiently - a testament to the power of learning through first principles.

Medical Student Example:

Let's take the example of a medical student studying the human cardiovascular system, who is particularly intrigued by the mechanism of blood clotting. The initial confusion might stem from the complex nature of the clotting process and how the various components involved interact to prevent bleeding.

From this confusion, the student will formulate several questions: How does the body recognize an injury site? What triggers the formation of a clot? How does the clot know when to dissolve? These questions indicate the first principles the student is trying to uncover — the basic physiological rules and mechanisms that regulate blood clotting.

The student then forms hypotheses based on their current understanding and the gaps they've identified: Perhaps the body recognizes a site of injury due to signals from damaged cells. Maybe the clotting process is triggered by specific chemicals released at the injury site. Possibly the clot dissolves when healing signals overpower the clotting signals.

To validate these hypotheses, the student studies the process in different scenarios: they delve into pathological conditions like Hemophilia (a disorder in which blood doesn't clot normally) or Thrombophilia (where clots form too readily). They look at the effect of certain medications like anticoagulants that prevent or slow down clotting. They also analyze how these processes differ between individuals of different ages, genders, or overall health.

With each scenario, the student's understanding deepens, leading to refined hypotheses and more targeted questions: What specific factors are missing or malfunctioning in Hemophilia that impede normal clotting? How do anticoagulant medicines interfere with the clotting process? Are there age-related factors that impact clotting efficiency?

Through this iterative cycle of confusion, questioning, and hypothesis testing, the medical student progressively uncovers the first principles of the coagulation process. This method, though arduous, equips them with the profound understanding necessary for their future medical practice, underlining the value of first principles in learning.

Exploring First Principles

First principles represent the foundational truths of any concept or discipline, stripped down to their most basic level. The beauty of first principles lies in their simplicity. They can be expressed using ordinary language, making them universally comprehensible. In essence, first principles are the building blocks of knowledge, the critical 'rules' that dictate how things work in each system.

What makes the idea of first principles particularly intriguing is their universality. These principles are not confined to a specific context within a given discipline, but rather they apply across that entire field of study. Whether it's physics, biology, economics, or architecture, each field is underpinned by its set of first principles. These principles serve as a guide, providing a clear and unambiguous framework from which more complex ideas and theories are built.

To illustrate the concept of first principles thinking, let's look at the approach of Richard Feynman, a renowned physicist known for his ability to distill complex scientific concepts into fundamental truths.

During his work on quantum electrodynamics, Feynman didn't just rely on the prevailing theories and methods of the time. Instead, he broke down the problem into its most basic elements.

Feynman questioned the very nature of particles and their interactions. He didn't accept the existing complex mathematical descriptions; he wanted to understand why particles behaved at the most fundamental level. This led him to develop what are now known as Feynman Diagrams. These diagrams weren't just another way to calculate things; they represented a completely different perspective on how particles interact.

This approach was more challenging than simply applying existing theories. Feynman had to confront the very foundations of physics, often finding himself at odds with established methods. However, this deep dive into the fundamentals led to a revolutionary understanding of particle physics. His work not only provided clearer insights into quantum mechanics but also laid the groundwork for many future discoveries. I encourage everyone to investigate Feynman's approach and brilliantly simple explanations for complex topics like physics and calculus which can be found on Google and YouTube.

Feynman's approach embodies the essence of first principles thinking - not accepting things at face value but digging deeper to understand the fundamental 'rules' at play. He didn't take the existing knowledge for granted; he dissected it to its core, leading to groundbreaking insights and methods. This kind of thinking often leads to creative, unconventional solutions.

The Value of Self-Discovery

In the quest for knowledge, the journey is just as crucial as the destination. It's easy to accept first principles at face value when they are simply handed to us, but the true value lies in the process of discovering these fundamental truths independently. This process of self-discovery is integral to a deep, robust understanding of any concept or discipline.

Why is self-discovery so crucial? When we actively engage in the process of learning - grappling with confusion, forming questions, developing hypotheses – we're not just passively consuming information. We're actively constructing our own understanding, connecting new knowledge to what we already know, and filling in gaps in our mental model of the world. This active involvement allows us to internalize the first principles in a way that a passive reception of information can never achieve.

Moreover, the process of discovering first principles independently fosters a mindset of critical thinking and inquiry. We learn to question the status quo, challenge accepted beliefs, and view problems from different perspectives. These skills are invaluable, not just for mastering a specific discipline, but also for evolving into more critical and effective thinkers.

While it's undoubtedly challenging to navigate the often-turbulent waters of confusion and uncertainty, it's these very challenges that stimulate cognitive growth. This struggle reshapes our neural pathways, strengthening our intellectual capabilities and fostering a lifelong love of learning. So, as daunting as the journey of self-discovery may seem, it's this very process that holds the key to deep, transformative learning.

Hypotheses as a Tool for Uncovering First Principles

In our journey of discovery, hypotheses serve as our guiding light, illuminating our path towards uncovering first principles. Hypotheses are our best-informed guesses - conjectures built upon our current understanding, aimed at revealing the foundational first principles that underline the concept at hand.

A hypothesis is not merely a static idea, but a dynamic tool that evolves and sharpens as we apply it in various contexts. Consider it as a key designed to unlock the door to understanding. As we use this key in different locks - that is, apply our hypothesis to varied, nuanced scenarios, and test it under different conditions - we learn more about its shape and structure, reshaping it and honing it to fit the lock of understanding more precisely. Each application serves to refine our hypothesis, to eventually reveal the true first principles.

As we delve deeper, applying and testing our hypotheses and considering additional parameters, they inevitably lead to more questions. These questions become increasingly specific and nuanced, honing in on the areas that our hypotheses have yet to fully explain. Each question, then, is like a miner's pick, chipping away at the mountain of superficial details and helping us dig deeper into the fundamental truths that we seek.

This continuous cycle of hypothesis formation, application, and refinement is the core of our journey towards first principles. It is akin to peeling back the layers of an onion, delving deeper until we reach the core. And just as the core of the onion is simple and unassuming, so too are the first principles we seek. Despite the complexity of the scenarios, we may consider and the intricacies of the hypotheses we may formulate, the ultimate goal is simple. The first principles, when unearthed, should be elementary truths that are expressed in the simplest language, unambiguous and comprehensible to anyone who seeks to understand.

This iterative process, therefore, is not just about learning for the sake of knowledge, but about stripping away the complex and often confusing superficial layers of a concept to reveal the simple, foundational truths that lie beneath.

Creativity Unleashed by Understanding First Principles

As paradoxical as it may sound, the deep understanding of foundational truths - or first principles - is the very key that can unlock the door to creativity. By having a firm grasp on the basic tenets of any concept, we gain the flexibility to think beyond the established norms and conventions. This enables us to generate novel ideas and solutions.

When we understand first principles, we are not simply reciting learned knowledge. Rather, we are viewing the subject through a unique lens that reveals the underlying simplicity of complex systems. This paves the way for 'outside the box' thinking, since we are no longer confined by surface-level understanding or traditional ways of thinking.

Take, for example, the innovation brought about by the Wright Brothers in the field of aviation. The first principles they recognized were Bernoulli's Principle, which explains how air pressure changes can create lift, and Newton's third law, which explains how pushing air backward will create a forward thrust. With these foundational truths in hand, the Wright Brothers could think creatively about the design of an aircraft and eventually succeed where others had failed.

Another compelling example is found in the realm of computer science, where first principles thinking led to the creation of object-oriented programming. Developers understood that, at their core, complex software systems are built from simple components that interact with each other. This understanding gave rise to the concept of "objects" in programming, which encapsulate data and functions into reusable components, greatly simplifying the process of software development and ushering in a new era of programming.

In both cases, a deep understanding of first principles allowed for a level of creative problem solving that would not have been possible otherwise. The key is deconstructing the complexities to reveal the first principles which can then be reconstructed in a new way. When we anchor our understanding in the bedrock of foundational truths, we free our minds to explore the uncharted territories of creative thinking and problem solving. That's the true power of first principles - they don't just help us understand the world as it is, but envision and create the world as it could be.

Acceptance of Potential Limitations

As we delve into the journey of discovery, it's crucial to acknowledge the potential challenges that might arise. Despite our best efforts and the relentless application of confusion, questioning, and hypotheses, there may be instances where we are unable to identify the first principles independently. But let's be clear: this doesn't signify failure. On the contrary, it's a testament to the complexity of the subject matter and the richness of our learning journey.

Identifying first principles is not always a straightforward process. It involves peeling back multiple layers of understanding, constantly questioning what we think we know, and being open to the possibility of being wrong. It can be akin to navigating a maze with countless paths, each leading us deeper into the core of understanding. There can be moments of frustration, even desolation, when the path seems obscured or the answers elusive.

Yet it's in these moments that our resilience and determination are truly tested. Recognizing the challenge doesn't discourage us; instead, it fuels our resolve to press on, to keep questioning, hypothesizing, and testing until we reach that fundamental truth.

This acceptance of potential limitations is not about lowering our expectations, but about embracing the reality of the learning journey. It's about understanding that every question we ask, every hypothesis we formulate and test, brings us one step closer to the truth, even if it doesn't lead us directly to the first principles.

Moreover, accepting potential limitations fosters an environment where we can learn without fear of failure. It teaches us that the true value lies in the process of discovery itself, not just in the destination. Even if we don't always reach the first principles independently, we're still advancing our understanding, strengthening our critical thinking skills, and fostering a deeper appreciation for the process of learning. This attitude not only makes us better learners but also more resilient and adaptable individuals, ready to face any challenge.

Reflection and Learning from Missteps

Once we have finally unearthed a first principle, whether independently or through assistance, it becomes a beacon illuminating our past journey. It's a moment to pause and take stock, to look back on the path we've travelled, strewn with questions, hypotheses, trials, and errors. This retrospective gaze is not a passive reminiscing; it's an active process of reflection and learning, crucial for our development as learners and thinkers.

Identifying missteps is an integral part of this reflective process. They are not markers of failure, but signposts of our learning journey, each pointing to an area where our understanding was challenged, and ultimately, enhanced. Missteps offer invaluable insight into how we think, how we approach problems, and how we adapt when confronted with the unknown. By identifying and studying them, we can uncover patterns in our thought processes, recognize recurring obstacles, and devise strategies to overcome them in the future.

However, reflection doesn't stop at mere identification. The real learning lies in embracing these missteps, understanding their cause, and gleaning valuable lessons from them. It's not enough to acknowledge that we were wrong; we must understand why we were wrong. What led us to that erroneous hypothesis? Was there a gap in our knowledge, a bias in our thinking, or a misunderstanding of the challenge? These are the questions we need to ask ourselves in our reflective journey.

Embracing failures and missteps as integral parts of the learning process redefines the narrative of learning. It shifts the focus from the simple 'right' or 'wrong' to a more nuanced understanding of learning as a dynamic, iterative process. It reframes setbacks not as stumbling blocks, but as stepping stones leading us towards a deeper understanding and mastery.

So, let's celebrate our missteps, our wrong turns, our hypotheses that fell short. For they are the evidence of our striving, the testament to our curiosity, and most importantly, the catalysts for our learning. They form the stitches in the rich tapestry of our learning journey, each adding a unique thread to our ever-evolving understanding.

Embracing Confusion: The Value of Discomfort in Learning

Understanding Confusion: Where does Confusion Come From?

Confusion, in the context of learning, often signifies an encounter with the unknown. It's a signal that we've brushed against the boundaries of our understanding and ventured into unfamiliar terrain. While it can be disconcerting, confusion is not a mark of inadequacy, but an indicator that we are on the cusp of potential growth.

At its core, confusion stems from gaps or missing links in our understanding. Think of your knowledge as an intricate web of interconnected ideas and concepts. As we learn, we add more threads to this web, linking new information with what we already know. However, when we encounter a piece of information that doesn't readily connect with our existing web, it creates a gap. This disconnect is what triggers confusion.

Perhaps we're missing some fundamental concepts that bridge the gap, or maybe the new information contradicts what we thought we knew, creating a dissonance that needs to be resolved. These gaps can be vast or minuscule, straightforward or complex, but they all incite a similar response: disorientation, bewilderment, and sometimes even frustration.

It's crucial to remember that confusion is not a sign of incompetence. Quite the contrary, it's a testament to the learner's intellectual courage. It means you've dared to step outside your comfort zone, to challenge your preconceived notions, and to wrestle with ideas that are at first elusive. It's a sign that you're on the brink of intellectual growth, about to transition into a more nuanced, complex understanding of the subject matter. Embrace confusion not as a stumbling block, but as a stepping stone towards deeper learning.

Embrace Confusion

Confusion, while initially disconcerting, is a powerful tool in the learning process. It acts as a spotlight, illuminating areas of weakness or gaps in our understanding. Far from being a symbol of defeat, confusion signals an opportunity for growth and enrichment. Just as challenges and difficult times reveal our areas of weakness, confusion expose the edges of our comprehension.

When we find ourselves in the throes of confusion, it's an invitation to dive deeper. It is our sign to dissect our understanding, identify the source, and pose targeted questions that can help us bridge the knowledge gap. This is not an easy process—it requires tenacity, resilience, and the willingness to wade through ambiguity. It often requires us to confront our assumptions and misconceptions. However, this discomfort is a clear indicator that we're venturing into the unknown and, crucially, making progress. In diving deep into our own confusions and understanding it and the cause, we will come up questions that target the knowledge we need to acquire to resolve the confusion.

The learning process is not linear, and neither is our encounter with confusion. We create, encounter, and resolve confusion in an ongoing cycle of intellectual growth. This cycle involves a dynamic dance with confusion—moving forward, confronting confusion, wrestling with it, and eventually resolving it, only to move forward again into new, complex territories.

Sometimes, we might find ourselves revisiting the same confusion, but armed with fresh perspectives or new information. This revisiting isn't regression; instead, it offers us the chance to deepen our understanding, to refine our grasp of the concept at hand, and to layer our knowledge.

Confusion, therefore, is not a stumbling block—it's a doorway to new learning opportunities. To bypass or sidestep confusion is to bypass potential growth. Instead, we must dive into it, explore its depths, and emerge on the other side with a better, more nuanced understanding. It might be unsettling, but remember: learning is a journey, and confusion is simply part of the landscape. Embrace it, explore it, and most importantly, learn from it.

Navigating Uncertainty: Harnessing the Power of Confusion and Questioning

The Integral Role of Questions

Questions, like lanterns in the dark, are integral in our navigation of the vast landscape of uncertainty. They're not merely markers of curiosity, but essential instruments in our quest to understand our confusion and unearth the first principles. They act as compasses that guide us through the maze of confusion and into the heart of understanding.

Every step in our learning journey, every twist and turn in our exploration, should be punctuated by questions. These questions should not be superficial or cursory—they should probe deeply, challenging assumptions, pushing boundaries, and peeling back layers of complexity to reveal the fundamental truths that lie beneath. They are the essential tools we use to dissect, examine, and ultimately understand the nature of our confusion and to find the first principles.

The beauty of questions lies in their ability to create connections. They help us link disparate ideas, stitch together various concepts, and build a comprehensive, interlinked network of understanding. By asking questions, we move beyond merely memorizing facts to engaging in a dynamic, active learning process that fosters critical thinking and in-depth comprehension.

Remember, our goal is not just to find answers, but to deepen our understanding. In the pursuit of first principles, our questions must therefore aim to uncover these foundational truths, the encompassing rules that form the bedrock of every concept. Through asking incisive questions, we aim to understand our own confusion, and, in the process, strip away the superfluous to zero in on these basic principles. This process, while sometimes daunting, is immensely rewarding—it's the path that leads us from confusion to clarity, from uncertainty to understanding, and from complexity to simplicity.

So, when faced with uncertainty, don't shy away. Use your confusion as a starting point, and let your questions illuminate the path. They are the guideposts on your journey, leading you ever closer to the discovery of the first principles. Harness the power of your questions and embrace the adventure of learning.

Formulating Questions: The Craft of Inquiry

The art of forming questions is at the heart of our learning process. Here's a guide on how to frame these questions effectively:

1. Understand what you know and what you do not know

    A good starting point for forming questions is understanding your current knowledge landscape - recognizing what you know and, crucially, what you do not know. Understanding is like mapping out a puzzle, observing the pieces we have in place, and acknowledging the spaces where pieces are yet to be placed. This practice allows us to grasp the landscape of our knowledge, reflecting on what we've already learned and pinpointing the gaps that still need to be filled. This is more than simply accepting our ignorance; it's about actively identifying the areas of our knowledge that require further exploration, the missing links that need to be discovered, and the weaknesses that need to be strengthened. These gaps become fertile areas for learning, places of fruitful confusion where we can direct our inquiries. Understanding these areas allows us to ask more targeted questions, enhancing our efforts to uncover specific insights, principles, and truths. It can be uncomfortable, even intimidating, to acknowledge and investigate our knowledge gaps.

However, by viewing these not as daunting chasms, but as exciting challenges and opportunities, we can embrace this discomfort and leverage it as a powerful tool for learning. By understanding what we know and what we don't know, we establish an ideal starting point for generating impactful questions and diving into the enriching cycle of confusion, questioning, and hypothesis formation.

2. Look deep and understand your confusion

Examining our confusion with a critical, introspective eye can unlock an unexpected reservoir of understanding. This introspection involves a deep dive into the murky waters of our uncertainty, where we confront our confusion head-on, dissecting it and turning it over in our minds to reveal its various facets and intricacies. The aim is not to rid ourselves of this confusion hastily, but rather to understand it, to map out its terrain and identify its roots. This process can feel overwhelming, but it's in the depth of this confusion that the most enlightening questions often lie hidden. By peering into the core of our confusion, we uncover the nuances of our understanding and pinpoint the specific aspects that we find perplexing. These discoveries, in turn, equip us to formulate precise, incisive questions, tailor-made to address our confusion. Such questions serve as torches, illuminating the way forward, directing us towards the resolution of our confusion, and subsequently, the enrichment of our understanding. Hence, the process of deeply understanding our confusion is a crucial step in our learning journey, paving the way for effective questioning and successful problem-solving.

3. Aim for the fundamental first principles or the 'rules' that are always true

As we navigate through the haze of confusion, our questioning should ultimately be aimed at unearthing the first principles – the immutable, fundamental truths that persist irrespective of changing circumstances or specific instances. These first principles are the bedrock upon which complex ideas and systems are built, serving as universal 'rules' at the core of every concept. They offer us a sturdy foundation and provide consistent guidance as we delve deeper into a particular field. The goal of our questions should be more than merely resolving an immediate state of confusion. Instead, they should be designed as strategic tools, digging through layers of complexity to reveal these underpinning truths. When we direct our curiosity towards these first principles, we transcend superficial understanding and step closer to achieving a robust, comprehensive grasp of the concept in question.

4. Start with asking 'Why'

Start with asking 'Why', before you ask other questions. It sets a solid foundation for deeper understanding. It prompts introspection and encourages you to probe the underlying principles before moving on to the specifics illuminated by asking 'when', 'how', and 'what'. Always asking 'Why', a potent questioning strategy, can serve as a catalyst in unearthing foundational truths and principles underlying any concept. Probing with 'why' propels us to step out of the sphere of superficial comprehension and dive deep into the heart of the subject matter. This method, popularly known as the 'Five Whys', prompts us to continuously strip away the layers of complexity, thus enabling us to discover the basic tenets at the root of our confusion or question. We reach a point where we can't ask 'why' anymore, signifying that we've encountered a fundamental truth. By persistently asking 'Why', we expose the scaffolding that supports our understanding, allowing us to explore and grasp the simplicity underneath the intricate nature of the subject in question. The premise here is simple: Question everything, always.

5. Ask 'when', 'how', 'what'

The utilization of 'when', 'how', and 'what' can further sharpen our understanding and provide a more comprehensive view of the concept at hand. The question 'when' aids in delineating the temporal or situational contexts in which a principle applies, helping us comprehend its dynamics across different scenarios. 'How' allows us to delve into the functional aspects of the principle, casting light on the processes, methodologies, and mechanisms that underscore its operations. 'What', on the other hand, illuminates the diverse manifestations, forms, and applications of the concept, enabling us to grasp its multiplicity and versatility. Together, these queries, acting as powerful analytical tools, help to sculpt a more rounded, detailed, and holistic understanding of the concept, enhancing our capacity to apply it effectively across varied circumstances.

Remember, asking questions isn't about revealing ignorance; it's a tool for seeking understanding. Don't be afraid to admit what you don't know. Every question is a stepping stone in the learning journey. Embrace them and watch as your understanding deepens and expands.

Hypotheses Evolution: The Dynamic Journey Towards Fundamental Truths

The evolution of hypotheses is an intriguing and dynamic process. Remember that our hypotheses are directed to uncover the first principles. As we begin to apply our initial hypotheses across a broad spectrum of scenarios, they are effectively stress-tested. These hypotheses, assumptions, or predictions, based on our current understanding, are thrust into a myriad of situations. Each unique scenario provides an opportunity for these hypotheses to prove their worth - they either hold up under scrutiny, or their limitations are brought to light.

Now, when a hypothesis stumbles, it's important to remember that this isn't a failure, but rather a valuable insight. Every time a hypothesis doesn't fit perfectly, it provides us with invaluable data to revise and refine our understanding. With each adjustment, the hypothesis evolves, becoming more and precise – closer to the true first principles.

This continuous process serves as a guide, directing us towards increasingly refined and pointed questions. The evolution our hypotheses undergo illuminates the regions of understanding that require further exploration. As we delve deeper into these regions, our questions, inherently entwined with our ever-increasing comprehension, grow more intricate and targeted. Each new question hones in on a more precisely defined gap in our understanding. As our knowledge widens, so does our capacity to forge hypotheses of the first principles intended to bridge these gaps. These hypotheses, in turn, are continually tested, and refined as we encounter fresh challenges, prompting further cycles of questioning, understanding, and discovery. In this ongoing iterative process, each step forward lays the groundwork for the next, propelling us ever closer to our ultimate goal: a profound, nuanced understanding of the fundamental principles that underlie the world around us.

This process can be likened to an archaeological dig. At the start, the shovel and trowel might work at a larger scale, removing the top layers of soil. But as we get closer to the artifact - the fundamental truth or first principle - our tools and methods become finer and more precise. We work carefully and meticulously, knowing that a hasty move could miss the mark.

In this journey of inquiry and learning, every cycle brings us closer to the first principles. Each refined hypothesis and nuanced question takes us deeper into the subject, incrementally enhancing our understanding. The result is not just learning, but constructive learning - a process that continually builds on itself, deepening our comprehension with every step. Engaging in this continuous learning process is what ultimately shapes us into skilled, analytical, and proficient thinkers.

The Cycle of Hypothesis Creation and Refinement: A Catalyst for Learning

Using Resources for Confirmation

We use external resources to answer our questions. The process of learning is intrinsically tied to the act of confirmation, a stage where external resources play an indispensable role. These resources, which can range from books and research papers to extensive databases, serve as troves of accumulated knowledge. They must be navigated strategically. We must resist the temptation to attempt to soak up all the information. Instead, we should leverage them as instruments to answer our pointed questions and validate our hypotheses, not as wellsprings from which to indiscriminately draw knowledge.

Why shouldn't we attempt to soak up all the information from these resources? The idea is that our minds will only retain the information we actively seek. Therefore, we should know what we seek before we engage with these resources, ensuring the information has a clear purpose in our learning journey. There should be a question on our mind that the information can stick to. If we passively read through the vast amount of information, there isn't a need for the information yet - there is no relevance, and so our mind will not retain it effectively. We must create relevance first by asking a question that ideally is born from the confusion in encountering a challenge.

Approaching these resources should be a thoughtful exercise, characterized by pointed, refined questions. These queries should stem from our independent explorations, reflections, and confusions about the subject matter. The ability to effectively articulate these queries distinctly enhances our interaction with the resources, making it more active, efficient, and relevant. Instead of being overwhelmed by the vastness of the available information, we extract only what is required to quench our specific thirst for understanding that is relevant to the challenge at hand.

Under this strategic approach, external resources transform into guides that reflect the accuracy of our comprehension and provide a path for future exploration. They serve as a backdrop against which we can gauge the validity of our hypotheses and where to move forward. Each varied scenario and additional parameter we encounter provides a different angle of reflection, offering a more well-rounded assessment of our understanding.

In this process, these resources help us answer our questions, and check whether the first principles we've deduced from our hypotheses remain steadfast. The principles are subjected to a multitude of situations and tested under diverse conditions to ascertain their universality. Every successful validation or inconsistency aids in the evolution and refinement of these principles. This is how we use external resources effectively in the journey of learning - not just as a direct source of knowledge, but mainly as a facilitator in the process of discovery and understanding.

Overall, the act of confirming our hypotheses is integral to the learning process, and external resources play a vital role. Books, research papers, databases - all these resources exist as vast reservoirs of knowledge. However, our goal should not be to absorb all the information they contain but rather to use them as tools to validate or challenge our hypotheses. We should approach these resources armed with specific, nuanced questions arising from our own explorations or to validate or invalidate hypotheses. When testing hypotheses against varied scenarios and additional parameters, these resources reflect the accuracy of our understanding and can lead to further exploration in terms of new questions or new scenarios to test the hypotheses. They are confirmatory tools, used to verify if our deduced first principles hold true under these diverse conditions.

How to Read a Resource for Learning

There comes a point in our learning journey when we seek out external resources, but this should not be the start of our journey.

Rather, it marks a transitional stage - a move from forming hypotheses based on our understanding to confirming or refuting these hypotheses.

Two methods guide us in this stage: the Hypothesis Method and the Direct Method.

The Hypothesis Method involves formulating hypothetical answers to our questions based on our current understanding or our current hypotheses aimed at revealing the first principles. These conjectures are then validated, either through practical application and observing the outcomes or through corroborative reading. If an answer/hypothesis stands the test, it implies the soundness of our logical reasoning. However, a refuted answer/hypothesis is just as valuable. It signals a flaw in our logic, leading us to revisit our assumptions, correct our understanding, and continue actively learning. Both situations can lead to more questions and further consideration of new scenarios to see if our current or revised hypothesis would stand. What we gain from this active learning process imprints deeply, making the knowledge hard to forget.

The Direct Method, on the other hand, involves turning directly to resources with specific questions, skipping the step where we formulate our own hypothetical answers to our questions. The key is to consume information only when it's necessary to advance our understanding. Reading becomes an effortless act of learning when we only seek out what is relevant. The information we encounter makes sense as it directly addresses our confusion, leading to a sense of relief and clarity. However, once the questions cease, and confusion fades, so does the learning. At this stage, reading becomes more passive, but it may remain effective because our prior active learning has primed us to understand even those concepts we hadn't questioned before.

The Hypothesis Method involves creating potential solutions based on current understanding and then seeking confirmation, whereas the Direct Method seeks answers to specific questions without forming prior hypotheses.

When reading resources, the initial approach should be to validate or invalidate our hypothetical answers to our questions as well as our hypotheses aimed at revealing the first principles (**Hypothesis Method**) or answer specific questions (**Direct Method**). Only towards the end of learning a topic should we engage in more passive reading. This later stage of reading will not only make sense of everything but also reveal a depth of understanding beyond what's directly presented.

Chapter 3 Summary

Confusion, Questions, and Hypotheses: The Trio of Constructive Learning

- Introduction to the transformative power of embracing confusion, fostering questioning, and forming hypotheses in learning.

Unearthing Foundations: Identifying First Principles

- Understanding First Principles
    - Defining first principles as the foundational truths underpinning concepts. Learning involves peeling back layers of complexity to uncover these fundamental truths.
    - Emphasizing the iterative process of confusion, questioning, and hypothesis formation to uncover these truths.

Embracing Confusion: The Value of Discomfort in Learning

- Understanding and Accepting Confusion
    - Confusion is recognized as a necessary step in the learning process, indicating the edge of current understanding and prompting deeper inquiry.

- Strategies for Embracing Confusion
    - Offering techniques for leveraging confusion as a tool for engaging with challenging material and stimulating questions.
    - Suggests actively engaging with confusing material, questioning its aspects, and using it as a basis to explore unknown territory in the subject matter.

Navigating Uncertainty: Harnessing the Power of Confusion and Questioning

- The Role of Questions in Learning
    - Questions are tools that dissect confusion, connect new information to existing knowledge, and guide the learner toward uncovering first principles.
- Formulating Effective Questions
    - Providing a guide to crafting questions that probe deeply, challenge assumptions, and lead to the discovery of first principles.
    - Effective questions dig deep, challenge existing understandings, and are driven by genuine curiosity, leading to a profound exploration of the subject.

The Cycle of Hypothesis Creation and Refinement: A Catalyst for Learning

- Using Resources for Hypothesis Validation
    - Discussing the strategic use of external resources to validate hypotheses formed from confusion and questioning.
    - Learners use books, papers, and other resources not to passively absorb all available information but to seek answers to their specific questions and validate their hypotheses.

- Hypothesis Method vs. Direct Method
    - Comparing two approaches to engaging with resources: forming and testing hypotheses vs. seeking direct answers to specific questions.
    - The Hypothesis Method involves creating potential solutions based on current understanding and then seeking confirmation, whereas the Direct Method seeks answers to specific questions without forming prior hypotheses.
- Reading Strategies for Learning
    - Recommends approaching resources with specific questions or hypotheses in mind to facilitate focused and effective learning.

Key Takeaways:
- Embracing confusion, rigorous questioning, and hypothesis formation accelerates deep, constructive learning.
- Identifying and understanding first principles through this process solidifies foundational knowledge and enhances problem-solving skills.
- Active engagement with learning material, through targeted questioning and hypothesis testing, leads to more meaningful and lasting comprehension.
- Utilizing external resources effectively involves a strategic approach that prioritizes validation of learner-generated hypotheses and direct answers to specific inquiries.
- The journey through confusion to clarity is an iterative process that fosters critical thinking, adaptability, and a deepened understanding of complex concepts.

Chapter 4
Primed for Knowledge: Preparing the Brain's 'Shelf' for Learning

"Beware of unearned wisdom."
- ***Carl Jung***

As we deepen our exploration of effective learning strategies, we turn our attention to the brain's readiness for acquiring knowledge. Imagine your brain as a shelf that needs preparation and arrangement before it can aptly store books. It's similar with our minds; they need to be primed for knowledge, organized in a manner that facilitates effective learning. In this chapter, we unravel the critical elements that make our minds not only receptive to information but also effective in retaining and integrating it.

We begin with the fundamental step of creating a 'cognitive appetite'; exploring how the inherent human desire to accomplish a task or solve a problem and encountering gaps can spark our curiosity and drive our quest for understanding. Building on this, we consider how setting the right context and purpose can effectively stage our minds for the assimilation of new knowledge.

Then, we shift our focus to an aspect of learning often perceived negatively: making mistakes. Our aim is to reshape our perspective towards errors, viewing them as valuable opportunities that can enhance our brain's receptivity and memory retention. Throughout this chapter, we will discover how these distinct, yet interconnected, elements work in tandem to make our minds more conducive to learning, by enhancing the quality and endurance of our understanding.

Creating a Cognitive Appetite: The Need for Knowledge

Delving deeper into the learning process, it becomes evident that creating a 'need' for knowledge is ***the most essential step in this process***. This cognitive need or 'appetite' originates from the very human endeavor to accomplish a task or overcome a challenge. It sprouts from the soil of confusion and blossoms into questions that guide our journey towards the first principles. The answers we seek during this quest carry a profound significance - they are not isolated fragments of information, but pieces of a puzzle aimed at completing a specific challenge.

To elucidate this concept, let's revisit the hammer example from Chapter 2, which highlighted how plunging headfirst into a challenge, before assimilating the details, stimulates a cognitive 'hunger' for understanding.

In the scenario, we were trying to push a nail into a piece of wood. The challenge sparked an intrinsic need to understand how a hammer functions. What we were craving for was not just a generic understanding of the hammer but an insight that was directly linked to our current task. Our cognitive appetite was specifically brought on by the requirement of a tool that could produce the necessary power to drive the needle into the wood. The tool represents knowledge. The confusion created from the challenge will make us identify and crave the knowledge we need to continue with the task.

Herein lies the beauty of the learning process. The need for knowledge wasn't arbitrary or imposed. It was born out of a real-world challenge and was driven by a specific goal - to drive the nail into the wood. The need for the knowledge came organically as a part of the process, and the formalized learning objective to 'learn how to use a hammer' was accomplished without it ever being the focus. The questions we formulated were targeted towards understanding our confusion when presented with a challenge and lead us towards creating a cognitive hunger for the relevant knowledge. This goal-oriented curiosity and the confusion we experience form the driving force behind creating a cognitive appetite. They propel us on our quest for discovering the first principles, making the journey not just rewarding but incredibly fulfilling.

Analogy: Building Muscle

Imagine you're embarking on a fitness journey, aiming to build muscle. This process serves as a fitting analogy for our concept of "creating a need" in learning.

In this scenario, going to the gym and engaging in weightlifting or resistance training represents the initial phase of tackling a challenge. When you lift weights, which are *heavier than you can comfortably manage*, you put your muscles under stress, creating tiny micro-tears in the muscle fibers. This is akin to diving into a problem or task without having all the necessary knowledge or skills - you're actively engaging and identifying the areas where you're lacking, creating confusion. While this may be to a point of frustration, it marks the beginning of the learning process.

After your workout, your muscles are primed and in need of repair. This is where protein intake becomes crucial. Consuming protein after your workout is like acquiring the specific knowledge after recognizing your gaps while tackling a challenge. The protein goes directly towards repairing and building the muscle fibers you've stressed during your workout. The muscles have created a 'need' for protein, and when it's provided, it's used efficiently and effectively.

Now, let's consider the opposite approach. If you were to consume copious amounts of protein without working out first, much of it wouldn't be utilized effectively by your body. In the absence of muscle stress and micro-tears, the body has no immediate use for the excess protein, and it is simply excreted. This parallels the idea of accumulating knowledge without first creating a need for it through practical application. Just as the body excretes excess protein, the mind may not retain knowledge that hasn't been anchored to a real-world problem, challenge, or question.

In learning, just like in muscle building, the sequence and timing are crucial. Facing a challenge or problem head-on before feeling fully prepared "exercises our mental muscles," creates a genuine need for the knowledge necessary to overcome it. Then, introducing the necessary 'nutrients' or knowledge afterward allows for effective assimilation and growth. This approach ensures that the new knowledge, like the protein, is not wasted but is utilized to build stronger, more capable 'muscles' of knowledge that can be used for problem solving. With more capable 'muscles', you can then tackle a larger challenge or problem and the cycle continues.

Setting the Stage for Assimilation: Establishing Context and Purpose

In our endeavor to make learning an enriching process, a pivotal step is setting the stage for the assimilation of knowledge - a task that involves establishing a clear context and a pertinent purpose for the information we pursue.

Context serves as the foundational canvas of our learning journey. It represents the broader narrative within which a piece of information finds its place. When we assign context to our learning process, we essentially create a mental structure that accommodates and organizes new knowledge, providing it a sense of belonging within the wider framework of our understanding.

Purpose, meanwhile, gives the information a clear sense of direction. A well-defined purpose sharpens our learning trajectory, serving as a compass that keeps our learning journey aligned. Understanding the purpose of information allows us to logically determine how knowledge is relevant to specific tasks, focusing on a detailed analysis of a concept's application and providing a clear, practical path for its use in real-world situations.

When we undertake a specific challenge, this context and purpose setting process unfolds almost automatically. It's a process intrinsically linked to the nature of problems and the human response to them.

When we confront a complex problem, we're plunged into a particular context. The problem, by its nature, defines the boundaries and conditions - the context - within which we must operate. Concurrently, the problem itself morphs into our purpose. It presents us with a clear objective - solving the problem - and consequently impels us to seek relevant information and broaden our understanding.

The beauty of this process lies in its self-propelling nature. Our intent to solve the problem automatically triggers a search for knowledge. This exploration, driven by context and purpose, enhances our comprehension and builds our capacity to understand and solve similar problems. It paves the way for an active learning process where the brain effortlessly and adeptly organizes and integrates new information, leading to profound understanding.

The act of setting context and purpose primes our cognitive faculties for the efficient and effortless absorption of knowledge. It makes our brain a fertile field where the seeds of knowledge can sprout and thrive. It encourages the establishment of connections, the discernment of patterns, and the extraction of insights, transforming the learning process into a captivating journey of intellectual discovery. Through the course of this journey, the seemingly complicated web of information unravels, presenting a clear, understandable picture that satiates our cognitive appetite and stokes the fire of curiosity, propelling us on our path of exploration.

Embracing Errors: The Role of Mistakes in Learning

The role of mistakes in learning is far more substantial than simply signaling a misunderstanding or a misstep. In fact, making mistakes during the learning process can spark a potent enhancement in our cognitive receptiveness and memory retention. Each mistake presents a rich opportunity to deepen our understanding, refine our skills, and optimize the way our brain learns.

A mistake highlights a gap or a misunderstanding in our knowledge. This serves as a catalyst, prompting us to home in on the area of difficulty. Our brain, alert to this gap, becomes primed for absorbing new information. This state of readiness can be likened to a cognitive sponge, eager to soak up the relevant knowledge to address the identified error.

The interesting facet of this process is that our brain is particularly receptive to learning after making a mistake. This cognitive shift is not merely about filling a knowledge gap but is a response to a deeper mechanism. The act of making a mistake stimulates our brain in a way that learning without errors does not. It creates a unique state of alertness that enhances the acquisition of new information. In this state, our brain is more efficient at processing and retaining information associated with the error than it would be when encountering the information for the first time.

Upon rectifying the mistake, we create a mental association between the error and the correction. This strong connection aids in the recall of the correct method or information in the future, turning the initial mistake into a powerful memory marker.

The cycle of making mistakes, becoming cognitively receptive, and then absorbing corrective information serves as a potent learning accelerator. It transforms the way our brain processes and retains new knowledge, optimizing our overall learning efficiency.

While I may not have empirical evidence to substantiate this claim, it is a notion drawn from my personal learning journey. There's something particularly resonant about the process of grappling with a problem, making an error, and then encountering the correction. Even when the rectification is understood passively, such as reading the correct answer, it tends to root itself firmly in my cognition. And if the resolution to the problem is actively sought, the learning experience becomes even more profound and enduring. This pattern, recurrent in my personal experiences, underscores the transformative power of mistakes in enhancing learning and memory retention.

I believe many of you might find this perspective relatable and insightful. It's a common understanding that making mistakes is part of the learning process. So, let's capitalize on this notion - aim to make as many mistakes as possible, as soon as possible. For those with whom this approach doesn't immediately resonate, I encourage you to apply it in your own learning endeavors and observe the outcomes for yourself. The real testament of its efficacy lies in personal experimentation and the insights gained from an experiential process.

I want to draw a parallel here to a concept discussed in Chapter 3, "Confusion, Questions, and Hypotheses: The Trio of Constructive Learning." Just as mistakes inevitably lead us to question where we went wrong, remember that confusion also serves as a catalyst for inquiry. Mistakes and confusion, though often met with dismay, play a pivotal role in the learning process, acting as catalysts for inquiry and reflection. When we make a mistake, our instinctive response is to question, "Where did I go wrong?" Similarly, confusion disrupts our understanding, compelling us to ask, "Why don't I understand this?" Both scenarios, as distinct pathways, converge at the crucial juncture of questioning, highlighting their integral role in constructive learning. This shared capacity to provoke thought and introspection underscores why embracing both mistakes and confusion is essential for deepening our understanding and advancing our knowledge.

Embracing this paradigm shift towards valuing mistakes as powerful learning tools paves the way for a more constructive and resilient approach to acquiring knowledge. We start to see each mistake not as a setback but, when viewed through the lens of opportunity, as a stepping-stone towards deeper comprehension and lasting retention. This evolution in perspective not only equips us with the fortitude to boldly venture into new territories of learning but also imbues us with the understanding that every mistake—while offering a chance to correct an error—is, in fact, a guidepost leading us towards intellectual growth and mastery.

Chapter 4 Summary

Creating a Cognitive Appetite: The Need for Knowledge

- Learning initiates from a 'need' for knowledge, triggered by task-oriented challenges.
- This cognitive 'appetite' spurs the search for specific, problem-solving knowledge.

Setting the Stage for Assimilation: Establishing Context and Purpose

- Context and purpose, essential for learning, frame the broader narrative of new information.
- They often naturally emerge when facing a problem or challenge.

Embracing Errors: The Role of Mistakes in Learning

- Mistakes enhance cognitive receptiveness and memory retention.
- They alert our brains to knowledge gaps and stimulate a unique state of alertness for learning.
- Rectifying mistakes creates strong mental associations that aid future recall.

Chapter 5

The Learning Journey: Making Knowledge Acquisition Inevitable

> *"I asked for strength and God gave me difficulties to make me strong.*
> *I asked for wisdom and God gave me problems to solve.*
> *I asked for prosperity and God gave me brain and brawn to work.*
> *I asked for courage and God gave me dangers to overcome.*
> *I asked for love and God gave me troubled people to help..."*
>
> **- Hazrat Inayat Khan**

In the labyrinth of learning, how we approach challenges dictates the efficiency and efficacy of our knowledge acquisition. This chapter delves into the intricate dance between the challenges we undertake and the resulting learning that unfolds. It posits that active, goal-oriented challenges, which are specific in nature and often stretch our cognitive boundaries, serve as formidable catalysts, sparking an organic and inevitable learning process. Beyond merely absorbing information, learners are urged to immerse themselves in problems, to question, hypothesize, and discern first principles. Knowledge is not an end goal but a tool, a means to navigate and solve challenges. As we explore further, we'll unravel the potency of such an approach and provide concrete examples that demonstrate its transformative power in the realm of learning. This is how we can make knowledge acquisition not just more possible, but inevitable.

Specific Goal-Oriented Challenges: Catalysts for Active Learning

The bedrock of a successful learning journey often lies in the challenges we choose. Specific, goal-oriented challenges can act as potent catalysts for active learning. The power of these challenges stems from a combination of key characteristics, which, when appropriately designed, set the stage for the most effective knowledge acquisition.

Firstly, the specificity of the challenge is critical for creating an effective learning environment. Ambiguity can lead to unfocused efforts and inefficient learning, while a clear and specific challenge provides guidance and direction. It narrows down the broad field to a specific set of skills and understanding needed for the task at hand. For instance, instead of aiming to learn about medical emergency protocols, a medical student could target mastering protocols related to cardiac arrest, facilitating more effective learning and application. Moreover, the specificity of challenges enables accurate progress mapping, contributing to motivation and maintaining engagement in the learning journey. Therefore, a specific challenge is both a beacon and a roadmap, illuminating the learning path and providing clear milestones, fostering efficient and satisfying learning.

Secondly, when embarking on a learning journey, challenges must be goal-oriented, surpassing a mere 'understanding' level and involving higher-order functions like 'creating', 'evaluating', or 'analyzing', according to Bloom's Taxonomy. A significant method of achieving this is to direct learning towards the creation of something tangible, which calls for a multi-tiered cognitive process. The emphasis is choosing a challenge that mirrors the final application of the knowledge you're seeking, intertwining the learning process with a practical, real-world application. This approach transforms passive information absorption into an active process, embedding context, and purpose into the learning. The knowledge acquired through such challenges is more integrated, enabling learners to apply their knowledge across varied contexts, reinforcing understanding, enhancing memory retention, and fostering cognitive adaptability. In essence, to optimize learning, focus on creating something concrete that reflects the ultimate application of the knowledge, thus making learning an active, engaging, and rewarding experience.

Thirdly, selecting challenges that extend beyond our comfort zones is essential to a more dynamic learning process. When a task or problem is too straightforward, it lacks the tension necessary to stimulate confusion, curiosity, and provoke in-depth exploration, thus rendering the learning passive and superficial. In contrast, taking on a challenge that pushes our cognitive boundaries forces us to grapple with unfamiliar concepts, encouraging us to think critically, formulate hypotheses, experiment, and learn from our mistakes. This mental exertion leads to a heightened state of cognitive receptiveness, making our brain more attuned to absorb and integrate new information. Importantly, it is this struggle through uncertainty and complexity that ignites our cognitive appetite, spurring us to dig deeper and understand better. Stepping out of our comfort zone propels us into a state of active learning, fostering intellectual growth and paving the way for substantial knowledge expansion.

Fourthly, we must embrace the courage to undertake challenges before we feel prepared or have acquired complete knowledge on the topic. This strategy, while seemingly counter-intuitive, propels us into a cycle of active, experiential learning. Diving headfirst into a challenge with knowledge gaps causes confusion and ignites a potent cognitive appetite. This hunger, born out of necessity to resolve the challenge and the resulting confusion, impels us to actively seek, question, and readily absorb the requisite information. This process, often characterized by a heightened state of focus and curiosity, enhances our brain's receptivity to new information, facilitating more efficient knowledge assimilation and retention. Moreover, it allows us to experience first-hand the practical implications and applications of theoretical concepts, thereby making our learning more contextually relevant, enduring, and impactful.

Lastly, the process of tackling challenges necessitates measured evaluation and feedback. This integral component of the learning journey allows us to gauge our progress, identify our strengths and weaknesses, and modify our strategies. Without regular evaluation and constructive feedback, our learning could veer off course, and the inaccuracies could go unnoticed and uncorrected. Feedback, both self-generated and external, fosters a loop of continuous improvement, enabling us to recalibrate our approach, focus our efforts, and ultimately enhance our learning efficiency. It provides the insight we need to refine our strategies and evolve our understanding, facilitating continuous progress towards our learning goals. Regular, focused feedback thus serves as the compass that navigates our learning journey, steering us towards the effective acquisition of knowledge and skills.

Careful attention should be paid to avoid some common pitfalls. Avoid setting too broad or too easy challenges, as they do not facilitate active learning. Shying away from starting before feeling ready or starting with having all the required knowledge can also hamper the learning process. Furthermore, selecting challenges that do not mirror real-world applications can lead to learning that feels abstract and disconnected, reducing its long-term retention and application. Instead, always strive for specificity, goal-orientation, adequate difficulty, early initiation, real-world relevance, and feedback when designing your learning challenges.

Designing Effective Challenges - Practical Examples

Let's bring the principles of specific goal-oriented challenges to life by examining an example from medical education. In this field, simulation-based training is a powerful tool that enables learners to apply new information immediately, even before achieving full comprehension. A medical student learning about emergency response might participate in a high-fidelity simulation of a patient in cardiac arrest. This specific challenge focuses the student's learning efforts on understanding and applying cardiac arrest protocols. It is goal-oriented, as the student's immediate objective is to save the simulated patient's life.

Importantly, the simulation extends the student beyond their comfort zone, especially if they have just been introduced to the protocols or not at all. They are forced to apply their rudimentary understanding and make split-second decisions, which may feel uncomfortable and overwhelming. Yet, this tension provides a potent stimulus for active learning. The immediate application of their nascent knowledge creates a cognitive dissonance that prompts pointed, practical questions about the protocol.

The student is immersed in this scenario before feeling fully ready or having complete knowledge about cardiac arrest protocols. This cognitive leap creates a drive to fill their knowledge gaps, spurring active learning. After the simulation, they delve deeper into the theoretical aspects, integrating their experiential learning with theoretical knowledge. This process of starting before ready and iterating their understanding through practice and reflection is a powerful catalyst for knowledge acquisition.

Feedback plays a crucial role. Instructors provide real-time feedback during the simulation, while post-simulation debriefings offer reflective feedback on the student's performance. This evaluation and feedback, combined with the student's self-reflection, contribute to identifying areas for improvement and adjusting future learning efforts.

The simulation scenario is a concrete, real-world application of the cardiac arrest protocol knowledge. It transforms the passive acquisition of theoretical knowledge into an active process, where the student learns by doing. Moreover, it promotes the internalization of the protocols, equipping the student with the confidence to apply them in real-world situations.

However, the learning process would be less effective if the challenges in the simulation were too broad or easy. If the student waited until they felt ready or had full knowledge before beginning, the stimulus for active learning would be diminished. If the simulation did not mimic a real-world application, the student's learning might feel abstract and disconnected.

In conclusion, this medical simulation example demonstrates the power of specific, goal-oriented challenges as catalysts for active learning. It incorporates the principles of specificity, goal orientation, comfort zone extension, early initiation, and real-world application, with measured evaluation and feedback guiding the learning journey. Through such challenges, the medical student not only learns about cardiac arrest protocols but also develops the confidence and capability to think critically and apply the protocols in real-world situations, reinforcing the principles underpinning effective knowledge acquisition.

Here is another example that explains the appropriate design of an effective challenge:

In learning a new language, specific challenges tailored to real-life applications, akin to medical students' high-pressure simulations, can significantly enhance active learning. Take, for example, a beginner in Spanish navigating Madrid for a day, committed to communicating only in Spanish. This immersive challenge directly reflects the ultimate goal—fluency in real-world situations.

The challenge's specificity lies in practical tasks like ordering in cafés or seeking directions, focusing the learner on conversational Spanish. Being unprepared heightens cognitive engagement, turning each interaction into a real-time learning opportunity. Mistakes, while expected, become valuable lessons driven by the necessity to communicate.

Feedback is instantaneous within the natural flow of conversation, with each successful exchange reinforcing correct usage and any miscommunication highlighting areas for improvement. A friend fluent in Spanish can enhance this learning cycle by offering immediate corrections and encouragement, further embedding the language through practical use.

By the day's end, much like the medical student in simulation training, the learner emerges with a practical understanding of Spanish, born from a challenge that mirrors the authentic application of speaking fluently. This example illustrates how specific, real-world challenges can make learning a language not just achievable but inevitable.

Challenge: Language Student Communicating in Spanish in Madrid for One Whole Day

- **Specificity**: The challenge targets specific tasks like ordering in cafés or asking for directions in Spanish, focusing the learning on essential conversational skills.

- **Goal-Oriented**: Beyond understanding, the challenge requires applying Spanish in real situations, pushing the learner to use higher cognitive skills like analyzing and creating sentences.

- **Extending Comfort Zones**: Navigating Madrid in Spanish extends the learner beyond their comfort zone, encouraging critical thinking and problem-solving in unfamiliar language situations.

- **Starting Before Ready**: The learner tackles this challenge with potential gaps in their Spanish knowledge, learning through practical use and immediate necessity.

- **Evaluation and Feedback**: Real-time feedback comes from the outcomes of conversations, with successful interactions validating learning and misunderstandings highlighting areas to improve. In addition, the friend is there to help and give specific feedback.

- **Avoiding Pitfalls**: The challenge is neither too broad nor too easy, focusing on practical tasks. It encourages early initiation and ensures real-world relevance by situating the learning experience in Madrid, directly tying the learning to practical use.

Learning as a Natural By-Product of Completing the Challenge

The act of completing a challenge often yields a profound yet unexpected reward: the acquisition of knowledge as a natural by-product. This approach centers on identifying and understanding the knowledge gap through the challenge. The question, "What do I need to solve this problem?" pinpoints the knowledge gap, identifying the missing 'tool' needed to resolve the challenge. Recognizing and truly understanding this gap before seeking the information is crucial, as it creates a learning necessity.

As learners tackle challenges, they're propelled by confusion and curiosity rather than rote memorization, leading to the discovery of the essential principles needed to understand and solve problems. This process not only fills knowledge gaps but also makes the assimilation of new information seamless and purposeful. This underscores a fundamental truth about human cognition. We are wired to learn most effectively when engaged in meaningful challenges that demand more than we can handle comfortably. Challenges are the beginning of the learning process, from which knowledge emerges as a natural consequence of our endeavors to achieve, solve, and conquer. This makes learning inevitable.

Chapter 5 Summary

Overview

- Investigates how active, goal-oriented challenges can foster deeper learning.
- Advocates for hands-on engagement with challenges to incite questioning, hypothesizing, and understanding first principles.
- Treats knowledge as a tool to navigate and address challenges rather than an end goal.

Specific Goal-Oriented Challenges: Catalysts for Active Learning

Introduction

- The foundation of effective learning is in specific and goal-oriented challenges.
- Specific challenges aid in focusing the learning process and allowing for clearer progress mapping.
- Goal-oriented challenges require higher cognitive functions, promoting better integration and application of knowledge.

Characteristics of Appropriate Challenges

- Specificity
    - Facilitates focused learning and clear guidance.
    - Helps in establishing precise milestones and maintaining engagement.
- Goal-orientated
    - Promotes higher-order cognitive engagement according to Bloom's Taxonomy.
    - Encourages the creation of something tangible.
- Stretching cognitive boundaries
    - Encourages critical thinking and deep exploration.
    - Fuels the cognitive appetite for deeper understanding.

- Courageous engagement
    - Encourages diving into challenges even without complete preparation.
    - Facilitates experiential learning and contextual understanding.
- Evaluation and feedback
    - Necessary for identifying strengths and weaknesses.
    - Facilitates continuous improvement and steering towards effective knowledge acquisition.
- Pitfalls to avoid
    - Broad or easy challenges, delay in starting, challenges not grounded in real-world applications.

Designing Effective Challenges - Practical Examples

Overview
- Illustration of the principles through a medical education example.

Conclusion
- Emphasizes the transformational power of specific, goal-oriented challenges in learning.

Learning as a Natural By-Product of Completing the Challenge

- Identifying and understanding the knowledge gap is central to this learning approach.
- Human cognition is optimized when we engage in meaningful, challenging tasks.
- Facing challenges initiates the learning process, with knowledge acquisition as a natural outcome, ensuring learning is an inevitable process.

Chapter 6
Harnessing the Power of AI in Modern Education

"A sword is only as good as the man who wields it."
- George R.R. Martin

In the annals of history, transformative technologies have reshaped industries and redefined paradigms. One such game-changing force in the realm of education is Artificial Intelligence (AI). While traditional pedagogical methods have often been bound by uniformity, leaving little room for the multifaceted nature of individual learning, AI emerges as a beacon of personalization and efficiency. At the forefront of this evolution is the promise of 24/7 assistance, the rapidity of instantaneous feedback, and an invigorated shift towards a student-centric approach.

As we delve deeper into this chapter, we will explore the revolutionary capabilities of tools like ChatGPT, illuminating their role in problem understanding, hypothesis creation, and the distillation of complex ideas. Moreover, as we prepare to navigate the brave new world of AI-driven education, it becomes paramount to not only embrace its potential, but also recognize and mitigate its limitations. The horizon of educational prospects glows brightly, hinting at a future where each student's journey is as unique as their own fingerprint, all thanks to the harmonizing dance between AI and human individuality.

General advantages of using AI in Education

The advent of artificial intelligence (AI) is poised to herald significant changes in the educational arena. Historically, traditional educational models have operated on a largely uniform structure, often sidelining the unique needs of individual learners. However, AI brings forth a transformative shift from this model, ushering in a more dynamic and responsive educational framework.

Several unique advantages become evident when integrating AI into the educational sphere:

1. 24/7 Assistance: Traditional educational boundaries are constrained by time, but AI-powered platforms, like chatbots or intelligent tutoring systems, are always available. This continuous availability ensures that learners can seek assistance, clarification, or delve deeper into subjects of interest unhindered by temporal limitations. This bypasses the need to wait for professors, it saves the time from having to talk to professors about questions you may have (instead of asking questions, you can focus on more meaningful conversations or perhaps more intricate discussions on knowledge material) and gives a much simpler and more comprehensive approach compared to Google searches.

2. Speed: With AI, feedback is almost instantaneous, allowing learners to move forward without awaiting periodic assessments or delayed feedback. This nurtures a perpetually engaged learning environment, promoting consistent motivation and inquisitiveness. Having 24/7 assistance also contributes to this, no need to wait for people or go through the hassle of searching for the answers. Although searching for the answers can also provide its own benefits in the learning process, with AI, it can be more refined and not as excessive.

3. Student Driven: AI facilitates a transition from a predominantly teacher-centric methodology to a learner-driven approach. With AI's capabilities, learners exercise more control over their educational journey, handpicking subjects of intrigue, asking their own questions

based on their own curiosity and problems.

In the vast landscape of education, AI emerges as a powerful tool as well as a pioneering force, setting the stage for a more adaptive, immediate, and learner-centric educational experience.

How to use ChatGPT in the New Learning Paradigm

Artificial intelligence, specifically tools like ChatGPT, offer transformative methods of learning and understanding. Here's how ChatGPT can be seamlessly integrated into the learning process:

A tool for Understanding the Problem.

At the heart of the learning method lies the principle of comprehending the challenge at hand. This is not just a cursory step, but rather a foundational pillar for the rest of the entire process. Here is a summary of what we discussed previously in Chapter 2- How to Deeply Understand the Challenge:

Truly understanding a problem necessitates embarking on a multifaceted exploration. Initially, there's the stage of deconstruction and simplification. This step is about taking the complex, often bewildering challenges and dissecting them down to their very core elements, making connections clearer and eliminating any lingering ambiguities. Following this is the critical phase of state identification. In this stage, learners pinpoint the existing scenario, labeling it the 'initial state', while also painting a clear picture of the 'desired state' or ultimate objective. Between these two states lies the 'problem space', the gap or chasm that needs bridging. And finally, with a clear roadmap in hand, the learner reaches the phase of 'transformation recognition', which focuses on understanding the shifts, both big and small, required to transition from the present scenario to the envisioned one. This final step is all about strategy, pinpointing the crucial actions, and tactically executing them to achieve the solution.

But where does ChatGPT fit into this equation? ChatGPT can be employed as a tool to assist in breaking down problems, delving into each component, and understanding it in its most rudimentary form. By posing questions, seeking clarifications, or asking for examples, learners can leverage ChatGPT to gain a more nuanced understanding of each element of their challenge. In essence, it acts as a digital guide, helping illuminate the intricacies of the problem at hand.

Here is an example:

Using ChatGPT in Medical Studies: A Deep Dive into Understanding the Problem

The medical field, with its intricate pathologies and myriad of symptoms, can often present challenges that require a thorough understanding. Here, ChatGPT can be an indispensable ally. Take, for instance, the approach of breaking down clinical scenarios. When presented with a practice problem, simply transposing the question to ChatGPT can unfold a wealth of information. By prompting ChatGPT with a structured query like, "For the following clinical scenario, identify all the key symptoms and significant clues. Then, for each identified key symptom and significant clue, provide the underlying mechanism of how it can contribute to the patient's condition. Then for each key symptom/significant clue identified, provide a list of differential diagnoses," the user is essentially instructing the AI to think critically and methodically about the case.

This process reveals the power of structured thinking. ChatGPT doesn't just return an answer; it provides a step-by-step breakdown of the scenario. First, by identifying key symptoms and significant clues, it offers a summarized view of the case, enabling the student to distinguish between the most relevant information and any potential red herrings. Once these are pinpointed, delving into the underlying mechanisms offers a profound understanding of the pathology at play. This isn't just rote learning; it's the piecing together of the physiological puzzle that underpins the patient's condition.

Lastly, by listing differential diagnoses for each symptom or clue, ChatGPT showcases the vast interconnectedness of medical knowledge. Symptoms often don't point to a singular condition, and understanding the various possibilities is crucial in clinical decision-making.

ChatGPT serves as more than just a question-answering tool. It's akin to a digital tutor, guiding medical students through the maze of clinical scenarios, teaching them not just the answers but, more importantly, the structured thinking and deductive reasoning that's essential in the medical field. Through this method, ChatGPT doesn't just provide information; it instills a methodology, ensuring that students don't just know, but truly understand. This deepens comprehension, aids in recall, and ultimately helps mold more astute future physicians.

A tool for answering pointed questions

Summary of Using Resources to Guide Hypothesis Creation:

Learning hinges on the act of confirmation, using resources like books and databases. However, their vastness necessitates a purposeful approach, employing them to test our hypotheses. By framing focused questions based on our uncertainties, we extract essential information, transforming these resources into mirrors of our understanding.

Our learning adopts two main strategies: the **Hypothesis** and **Direct Methods**. In the former, we verify our knowledge-based assumptions against external resources, learning from each outcome. The Direct Method, however, has us approach sources with distinct questions, gleaning only relevant insights. Although our learning actively begins here, it can transition to a more passive mode, leveraging our base knowledge to understand new concepts.

ChatGPT as a Resolute Learning Ally:

In the evolving landscape of learning, traditional methods have witnessed significant transformations. Where once learners relied almost exclusively on books, they now have an arsenal of digital tools at their disposal. One of the most groundbreaking among these is ChatGPT. Instead of navigating through pages or skimming chapters in search of answers, individuals can now effortlessly pose questions directly to this platform. Moreover, the ability to upload entire books or PDFs, tapping into the capabilities of AI chatbots and GPT-4 plugins, has revolutionized the learning process. ChatGPT stands out by providing insights that are not just based on a singular chapter or a select passage but are rooted in the entire content of the uploaded material. This comprehensive approach ensures that learners gain a holistic understanding of their queries.

However, the brilliance of ChatGPT doesn't merely reside in its vast knowledge base. One of its most commendable features is the conciseness of the information. While the platform is adept at introducing learners to related concepts and ideas that might enrich their understanding, it also delivers information with limited yet appropriate volume. By limiting its responses to the essential context required to understand a given answer, ChatGPT ensures that learners are not overwhelmed by a deluge of information. Instead of being passive recipients of a torrent of details, users are encouraged to actively engage with the information, utilizing it as a tool to either validate or challenge their pre-existing hypotheses or answer pointed questions.

The dynamism of ChatGPT further manifests in the speed and efficiency with which you can operate it. For anyone in the throes of the learning process, the rapid hypothesis formation and refinement cycle is paramount. With ChatGPT, this cycle experiences a remarkable acceleration, enabling learners to rapidly zero in on foundational principles. The platform's inherent adaptability grants users the flexibility to test their hypotheses in a multitude of nuanced scenarios. This adaptability, combined with its speed and precision, makes ChatGPT not just a tool but a transformative ally in the quest for knowledge.

Ease of asking questions and getting answers

The simplicity with which one can pose questions to ChatGPT acts as a catalyst for stimulating even more queries. It is the ease of getting answer that allows us to effortlessly partake on this path of minimal resistance. Usually asking questions and looking for the answer in books or asking other people can be time consuming or difficult. Given that ChatGPT provides swift and lucid responses, each answer often motivates further curiosity. As one question gets resolved, it naturally paves the way for subsequent inquiries, fostering a continuous and enriching cycle of learning and exploration. Furthermore, and even more importantly, the process of investigating and understanding one's own confusion to then formulating a question is an essential part of the learning process which is is facilitated by the ease that AI provides.

A tool for finding simplicity

The prowess of ChatGPT lies not just in its vast repository of knowledge, but in its unique ability to distill and present that knowledge in a digestible manner. Complex concepts, which might span chapters or even entire books, can be synthesized by ChatGPT into concise explanations that maintain the core essence of the idea. You can even ask it, "explain it to a 10-year old" or "I don't get it, explain it in a different/simpler way". By navigating the intricate web of information and presenting it in a simplified format, ChatGPT acts as a bridge between advanced concepts and those venturing into a new subject. This ability to simplify without losing substance makes learning more approachable and less daunting, ensuring that users can grasp and build upon foundational concepts with confidence and clarity.

Preparing for the AI-Driven Educational Future

In the digital era, AI is not just a buzzword; it's a transformative tool set to revolutionize educational paradigms. However, like any tool, its efficiency depends on the proficiency of its wielder.

Despite the undeniable prowess of AI-driven tools like ChatGPT, users must be cognizant of potential inaccuracies in AI responses. While AI systems are built on vast data banks, they may sometimes yield answers that are less than perfect. This underscores the importance of critical thinking and cross-referencing in the modern learning process.

To harness the full potential of AI in education, it is imperative to bring about necessary shifts in the curriculum and teaching methodologies. Traditional pedagogical methods, tailored for rote memorization and standardized testing, might fall short in the face of AI's capabilities. Instead, the focus should be on fostering problem-solving abilities, critical thinking, and creativity.

Moreover, students must be instilled with adaptability and resilience. The digital world is in a state of constant flux, with technology advancements taking place at an unprecedented pace. In this context, a phrase of caution would be, "Don't let ChatGPT make you stupid." While AI can be a great helper, students should be encouraged to question, analyze, and validate information, ensuring that they are not over-reliant on any single tool.

In conclusion, as we stand at the cusp of this AI-driven educational frontier, it is essential to be prepared, adaptive, and forward-thinking. Embracing AI's potential while being aware of its limitations will pave the way for a more enriched and effective learning experience.

Potential for Customization and Scaling

Customization and scaling are perhaps the most transformative aspects of AI-driven education, bridging the gap between one-size-fits-all methods and personalized learning experiences. Envision a not-so-distant future where a student, instead of wrestling with generic educational content, interfaces with a chatbot specifically trained on the data or subjects they wish to delve into. What if students were given a chatbot with every textbook? Imagine the leap in engagement and understanding when every textbook is accompanied by its own dedicated chatbot, customized to guide and facilitate deeper exploration of the subject matter.

While this certainly means having AI systems with different data sets, it can also be about crafting an educational experience as unique as a student's fingerprint. The AI could also mold its interactions to approach subjects in a way that aligns with how the student best grasps concepts, making the learning curve less steep and more intuitive. This adaptive approach not only makes challenging subjects more understandable but also turns the learning journey into an enjoyable experience.

Moreover, a chatbot trained on specialized data doesn't just offer answers; it becomes an authority in that domain. Unlike broader AI systems which may sometimes spread themselves thin over vast realms of knowledge, these specialized bots hone in on their designated subject, offering depth and nuance. This meticulous focus drastically reduces the risk of inaccuracies or generalized answers, ensuring that the student receives precise and expert-level insights.

In essence, the future of education, empowered by AI, could very well be a harmonious blend of technology and human individuality. Every student would be equipped with an AI tutor attuned to their specific needs, propelling them towards unparalleled academic growth and exploration.

Chapter 6 Summary

Overview

- Revolutionizing Education with AI: Artificial Intelligence is transforming education by personalizing and streamlining the learning experience.
- Benefits of AI in Learning: AI offers significant advantages, such as continuous availability for learners and instant feedback, enhancing the learning process.

- The Role of ChatGPT: Tools like ChatGPT are instrumental in deciphering complex problems, aiding in hypothesis formation, and distilling intricate concepts into understandable formats.
- Integrating AI into Learning: Strategies for incorporating AI, like ChatGPT, into educational practices emphasize its utility in problem-solving and concept simplification.
- Preparing for an AI-Driven Future: Emphasizes the necessity for curricula to adapt to AI, fostering critical thinking and adaptability among students to fully leverage AI's potential.
- The Potential of Personalized Learning: AI, especially ChatGPT, stands to offer tailored learning experiences, making education more efficient, engaging, and suited to individual needs.
- Critical Thinking and AI Limitations: While AI opens new educational avenues, recognizing its limitations and fostering critical analysis skills in learners is crucial for effective use.
- A Vision for AI in Education: Envisions a future where AI-driven tools, tailored to individual learning styles, transform education into a more engaging and intuitive process.

Advantages of AI in Education

- AI transcends traditional time constraints, offering 24/7 assistance to learners for uninterrupted guidance.
- Instant feedback from AI accelerates the learning cycle, allowing for rapid progression and sustained engagement.
- A shift towards a student-driven approach in education is facilitated by AI, empowering learners to tailor their educational journey according to their interests and questions.

Utilizing ChatGPT in Education

- Problem Understanding: ChatGPT aids in decomposing complex problems into more manageable components, enhancing comprehension.

- Forming Hypotheses: Learners can use ChatGPT to explore various scenarios, testing and refining their hypotheses in real-time.
- Simplification: ChatGPT distills intricate concepts into more accessible explanations, bridging the gap between advanced subjects and learners new to a topic.

Navigating the AI-Driven Educational Landscape

- Critical thinking and validation are essential in an AI-enhanced learning environment to mitigate potential inaccuracies in AI responses.
- Curriculum and teaching methods must evolve to prioritize problem-solving, creativity, and critical thinking over rote memorization.
- Students should be encouraged to remain adaptable and resilient, developing skills to critically assess and question information, ensuring a balanced reliance on AI tools.

The Future of AI in Education

- Customization and Personalization: AI has the potential to offer tailor-made educational experiences, adapting to individual learning styles for more effective comprehension.
- Scalability: AI enables education to be scaled in a way that personalizes learning experiences without the traditional limitations of classroom sizes or resources.
- Specialization: Future AI tools could be developed for specific subjects or textbooks, providing expert-level assistance and insights in particular domains.

Chapter 7
Transforming Yourself

Face the challenge before you are ready. Use the knowledge before you fully acquire it. Knowledge is the tool, the objective is to overcome the challenge, the inevitable by-product is learning, and the end goal is to become a capable thinker. Through overcoming many challenges and solving many problems, we eventually become better at thinking about problems, solving them, and using our knowledge.

This knowledge eventually becomes more than just a tool to solve problems – it becomes an extension of our mind and shapes the way that we think.

It becomes the conduit that **expands** our mind's capability to think and create. We see more and do more. And through overcoming challenges, knowledge **transforms** the way we think. It transforms the way that we acquire more knowledge, dissect complexities, interpret nuances, adapt to new situations, balance intuition with logic, articulate our thoughts, understand and solve problems, envision solutions, perceive patterns, understand ourselves, utilize the first principles, harness creativity, and the way that we create.

Our goal as learners is not to accumulate knowledge. With every problem we solve, the better we get at using knowledge, our tool, to solve these problems. As we progress, knowledge becomes the conduit that expands, transforms, and elevates our cognitive ability and creative potential, and optimizes the way we harness them. As we elevate ourselves, we become people who can see more in that knowledge and do more - and create endless possibilities. As we elevate ourselves, we must then seek to solve greater problems.

Our goal is to become the best version of ourselves - to embrace the never-ending cycle of encountering challenges and overcoming them. In facing trials, we unveil the principles that define who we are. In mastering them, we inevitably grow. To shape oneself, one must sculpt their challenges.

In every endeavor no matter the size, start with audacious action, and trust that the next steps reveal themselves.

Index

A

Acquisition
  Knowledge acquisition, 25, 41, 56, 74, 95, 96
  Skill acquisition, 30, 45, 59, 123
Action
  Action plan, 18, 33, 51, 66, 67, 84
  Immediate action, 29, 38, 44, 85, 92, 123
  Action learning, 41, 55, 60, 78, 125
  Corrective action, 24, 37, 63, 99
Active
  Active learning, 42, 58, 81, 32, 65, 67, 111, 82, 85, 57
  Active process, 41, 67, 122, 96, 99, 114
  Active participation, 15, 45, 73, 32, 66, 91
  Active engagement, 42, 59, 85, 32, 65, 67, 111, 82, 85, 57
AI
  AI-driven, 33, 46, 72, 78, 84
  Applied AI, 38, 54, 91, 111, 129
  AI learning, 27, 61, 93, 124, 135
Approach
  Learning approach, 65, 78, 130, 67, 111, 125
  Teaching approach, 42, 67, 105, 96, 114, 129
  Practical approach, 15, 81, 122, 31, 98
  Iterative approach, 31, 66, 112, 89
Application
  Real-world application, 29, 41, 85, 66, 84, 124
  Practical application, 36, 62, 123, 91, 102, 129
  Clinical application, 45, 78, 102, 119, 128
  Theoretical application, 53, 91, 115, 123

B

Book
  Reference book, 25, 42, 73, 84
  Textbook example, 33, 57, 82, 94
  Guide book, 18, 42, 76, 98

C

Challenge
  Major challenge, 40, 64, 128, 84, 102, 129
  Significant challenge, 29, 46, 81, 91, 103, 117
  Ongoing challenge, 33, 55, 98, 94, 114
Cognitive
  Cognitive process, 34, 122, 83, 67, 91, 103
  Cognitive development, 45, 78, 119, 114, 125
  Cognitive load, 29, 65, 102, 96, 111
  Cognitive skills, 42, 75, 118, 31, 96, 129
  Cognitive ability, 18, 41, 67, 96, 111
Comprehension
  Reading comprehension, 29, 62, 98, 75, 94, 105
  Comprehension skills, 36, 75, 114, 91, 129
  Comprehension process, 41, 91, 123, 105, 112
Comprehensive
  Comprehensive approach, 42, 64, 118, 91, 112
  Comprehensive review, 33, 78, 122, 105, 128
  Comprehensive understanding, 45, 91, 102, 96, 123
Concept
  Concept development, 41, 65, 119, 96, 114, 129
  Basic concept, 33, 46, 81, 92, 105
  Fundamental concept, 29, 78, 125, 91, 112
Confusion
  Confusion arises, 29, 46, 78, 105, 128
  Confusion between, 33, 61, 105, 112
  Confusion about, 42, 68, 102, 114
Context
  Learning context, 42, 78, 116, 91, 128
  Social context, 41, 85, 128, 96, 125
  Context clues, 18, 67, 103, 92, 111
  Context-specific, 45, 91, 112, 105, 123
Creating
  Creating opportunities, 42, 67, 102, 96, 111
  Creating value, 41, 91, 128, 103
Critical
  Critical thinking, 32, 33, 129, 96, 102
  Critical skills, 18, 41, 81, 94, 114
  Critical analysis, 45, 78, 112, 103, 125
Curiosity
  Intellectual curiosity, 42, 78, 119, 96, 128
  Natural curiosity, 41, 91, 123, 67, 112
  Curiosity-driven, 29, 45, 79, 96, 105
  Encourage curiosity, 18, 67, 102, 91, 123

D

Deep
  Deep learning, 42, 78, 128, 96, 105
  Deep understanding, 33, 45, 102, 96, 129
  Deep knowledge, 29, 67, 91, 105, 112
Deeper
  Deeper understanding, 42, 66, 118, 96, 125

Deeper insight, 29, 78, 102, 96, 123
Deeper level, 45, 91, 123, 105, 112
Decision
   Decision-making, 41, 79, 119, 96, 129
   Strategic decision, 33, 45, 102, 105, 112
   Decision process, 29, 78, 112, 96, 128
Driven
   Driven by, 18, 67, 102, 96, 105
   Data-driven, 29, 78, 119, 91, 128
   Outcome-driven, 42, 91, 129, 96, 112

E
Education
   Medical education, 42, 79, 128, 96, 112
   Education system, 18, 67, 102, 105, 128
   Higher education, 29, 78, 119, 91, 123
Engagement
   Active engagement, 42, 59, 85, 32, 65, 67, 111, 82, 85, 57
   Student engagement, 41, 91, 128, 105, 112
   Meaningful engagement, 29, 78, 119, 96, 125
Engaging
   Engaging content, 41, 85, 110, 96, 128
   Engaging learners, 42, 59, 102, 96, 111
   Engaging in, 29, 78, 128, 105, 129
Experience
   Learning experience, 42, 59, 85, 96, 128
   Practical experience, 29, 78, 119, 91, 112
   Real-world experience, 41, 91, 128, 96, 123
Exploration
   Exploration process, 29, 78, 128, 91, 123
   Active exploration, 42, 67, 102, 96, 112
   Further exploration, 41, 85, 123, 96, 129

F
Feedback
   Continuous feedback, 42, 78, 129, 96, 123
   Instant feedback, 33, 59, 102, 105, 128
   Feedback mechanisms, 29, 67, 123, 91, 129

G
Gaps
   Knowledge gaps, 29, 79, 123, 96, 125
   Skill gaps, 42, 67, 102, 105, 128
   Addressing gaps, 41, 85, 119, 96, 112
Goal
   Learning goal, 42, 59, 119, 96, 128
   Goal setting, 33, 78, 129, 105, 123
   Specific goal, 29, 67, 102, 96, 112

H
Hypotheses
   Generating hypotheses, 29, 79, 112, 96, 129
   Testing hypotheses, 33, 67, 119, 105, 128
   Null hypotheses, 41, 78, 128, 96, 123

Hypothesis
   Working hypothesis, 29, 78, 119, 96, 128
   Hypothesis generation, 41, 91, 123, 105, 112
   Hypothesis testing, 33, 67, 102, 96, 129

I
Identifying
   Identifying gaps, 29, 67, 123, 96, 112
   Identifying problems, 41, 78, 119, 96, 128
   Identifying opportunities, 42, 59, 128, 105, 129
Immediate
   Immediate feedback, 41, 59, 128, 96, 123
   Immediate action, 29, 67, 102, 96, 128
   Immediate response, 42, 78, 119, 105, 129
Information
   Information processing, 41, 78, 119, 96, 123
   Relevant information, 29, 67, 102, 96, 128
   Information retrieval, 42, 59, 128, 105, 129
Innovation
   Innovation process, 29, 78, 119, 96, 129
   Technological innovation, 41, 91, 128, 105, 112

K
Knowledge
   Knowledge base, 29, 78, 119, 96, 125
   Knowledge transfer, 42, 91, 128, 105, 129
   Prior knowledge, 33, 67, 102, 96, 128

L
Learner
   Learner-centered, 29, 67, 128, 96, 123
   Active learner, 41, 78, 119, 105, 128
   Learner engagement, 42, 59, 102, 96, 123
Learners
   Adult learners, 42, 67, 128, 96, 123
   Engage learners, 29, 78, 119, 105, 128
   Support learners, 41, 59, 102, 96, 128
Learn
   Learn more, 41, 78, 128, 96, 123
   Learn about, 29, 67, 119, 105, 128
   Learn by, 42, 59, 102, 96, 129
Learning
   Active learning, 42, 58, 81, 32, 65, 67, 111, 82, 85, 57
   Deep learning, 42, 78, 128, 96, 105
   Experiential learning, 130, 42, 81, 58, 125

M
Making
   Decision-making, 41, 79, 119, 96, 129
   Meaning-making, 42, 78, 128, 96, 123
   Making sense, 29, 67, 102, 105, 129
Method
   Teaching method, 29, 78, 119, 96, 129
   Method of, 33, 67, 102, 105, 128
   Scientific method, 41, 91, 128, 96, 123

MAKE LEARNING INEVITABLE

Paradigm
  Paradigm shift, 45, 50, 55, 96, 128
  Learning paradigm, 29, 67, 119, 105, 129
  New paradigm, 41, 91, 128, 96, 123

P
Patient
  Patient care, 75, 77, 74, 96, 129
  Patient-centered, 29, 78, 119, 105, 128
  Patient experience, 42, 67, 128, 96, 123
Practical
  Practical application, 36, 62, 123, 91, 102, 129
  Practical skills, 35, 46, 53, 31, 96, 129
  Practical approach, 81, 122, 29, 96, 123
Principles
  Basic principles, 45, 91, 24, 96, 123
  Guiding principles, 33, 67, 102, 105, 129
  Foundational principles, 41, 91, 128, 96, 123
Process
  Learning process, 25, 43, 51, 96, 128
  Cognitive process, 122, 28, 41, 96, 123
  Iterative process, 45, 91, 78, 96, 128
  Decision-making process, 29, 79, 119, 96, 128
Problems
  Solve problems, 78, 128, 119, 96, 123
  Complex problems, 42, 67, 102, 96, 129
  Real-world problems, 41, 91, 128, 105, 123

Q
Questioning
  Questioning skills, 29, 78, 119, 96, 128
  Critical questioning, 41, 91, 128, 96, 123
  Questioning assumptions, 33, 67, 102, 105, 129

R
Real
  Real-world, 126, 47, 83, 96, 129
  Real experience, 41, 91, 128, 96, 123
  Real learning, 29, 67, 102, 96, 128
Resources
  Learning resources, 42, 91, 128, 96, 123
  Educational resources, 29, 78, 119, 105, 128
  Resource allocation, 41, 67, 102, 96, 129

S
Skills
  Critical skills, 42, 67, 102, 96, 128
  Practical skills, 35, 46, 53, 31, 96, 129
  Communication skills, 41, 91, 128, 96, 123

Solving
  Problem-solving, 42, 67, 102, 96, 128
  Collaborative solving, 29, 78, 119, 105, 128
  Solving complex, 41, 91, 128, 96, 123
Stage
  Developmental stage, 68, 70, 75, 96, 128
  Learning stage, 29, 78, 119, 96, 123
  Early stage, 41, 91, 128, 96, 129
State
  Current state, 41, 67, 102, 96, 128
  Desired state, 29, 79, 119, 96, 129
Step
  Next step, 29, 78, 119, 96, 128
  First step, 41, 91, 128, 96, 123
  Small step, 33, 67, 102, 96, 129
Student
  Student learning, 29, 78, 119, 96, 128
  Student engagement, 42, 91, 128, 105, 112
  Student-centered, 41, 67, 102, 96, 123
Subject
  Subject matter, 139, 54, 80, 96, 128
  Subject knowledge, 41, 91, 128, 96, 123
  Subject area, 29, 67, 102, 96, 128

T
Thinking
  Critical thinking, 32, 33, 129, 96, 102
  Creative thinking, 41, 78, 119, 96, 128
  Thinking skills, 42, 59, 128, 96, 129
Tool
  Learning tool, 60, 63, 136, 96, 123
  Assessment tool, 42, 78, 119, 96, 128
  Digital tool, 29, 67, 102, 96, 123
Traditional
  Traditional learning, 29, 31, 33, 96, 128
  Traditional approach, 41, 78, 119, 96, 123
  Traditional methods, 42, 67, 102, 96, 128

U
Understanding
  Deeper understanding, 42, 66, 118, 96, 125
  Clear understanding, 29, 78, 102, 96, 123
  Conceptual understanding, 45, 91, 123, 96, 112

W
Way
  Best way, 42, 78, 128, 96, 129
  Effective way, 29, 67, 102, 96, 128
  New way, 41, 91, 119, 96, 123

www.ingramcontent.com/pod-product-compliance
Lightning Source LLC
Chambersburg PA
CBHW030440010526
44118CB00011B/727